My name is

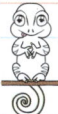

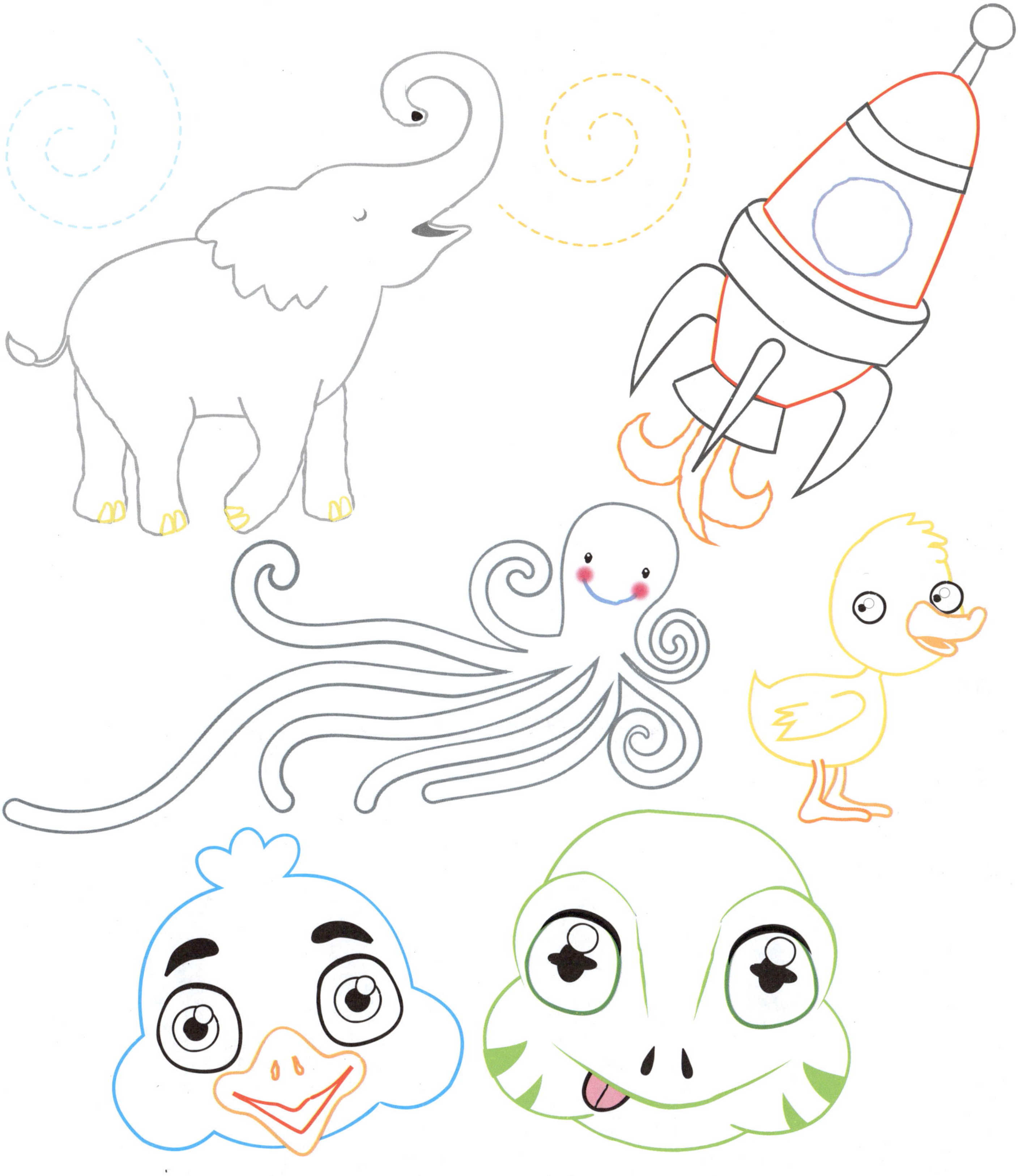

978-1-84654-932-8 **Prim-Ed Publishing** www.prim-ed.com

Cursive Letters

Trace the letters.

aA bB cC
dD eE fF
gG hH iI
jJ kK lL
mM nN oO

Complete the patterns.

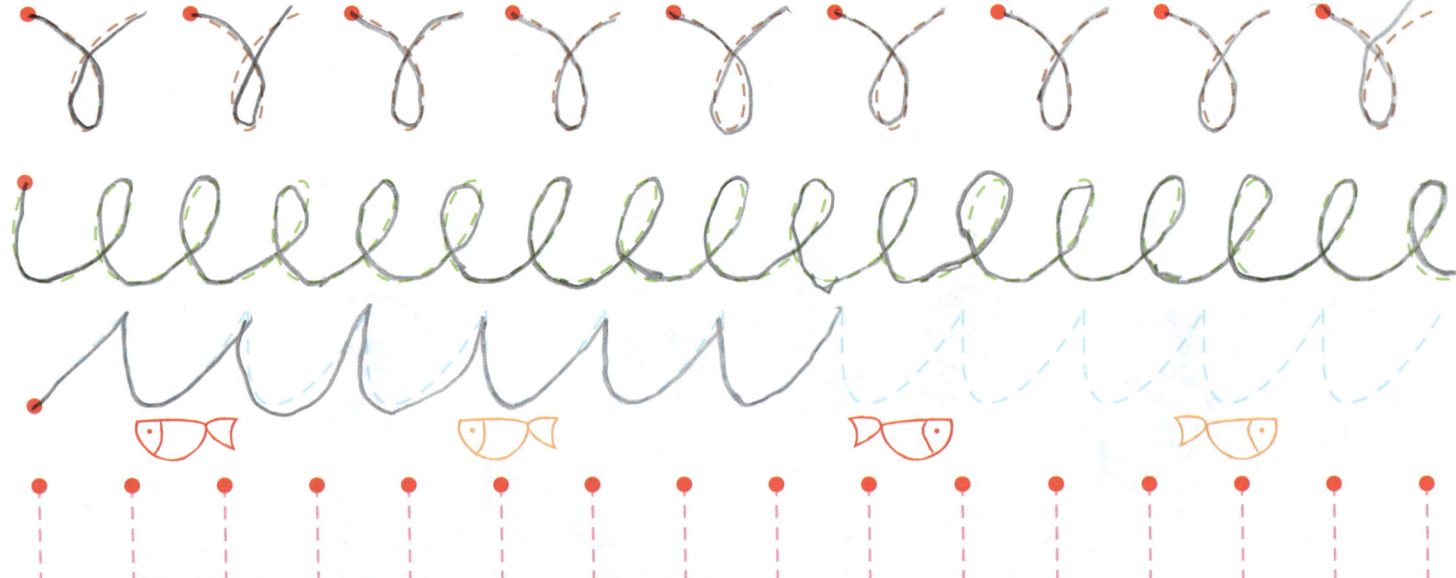

Cursive Letters

Trace the letters.

pP qQ rR
sS tT uU
vV wW xX
yY zZ

Complete the patterns.

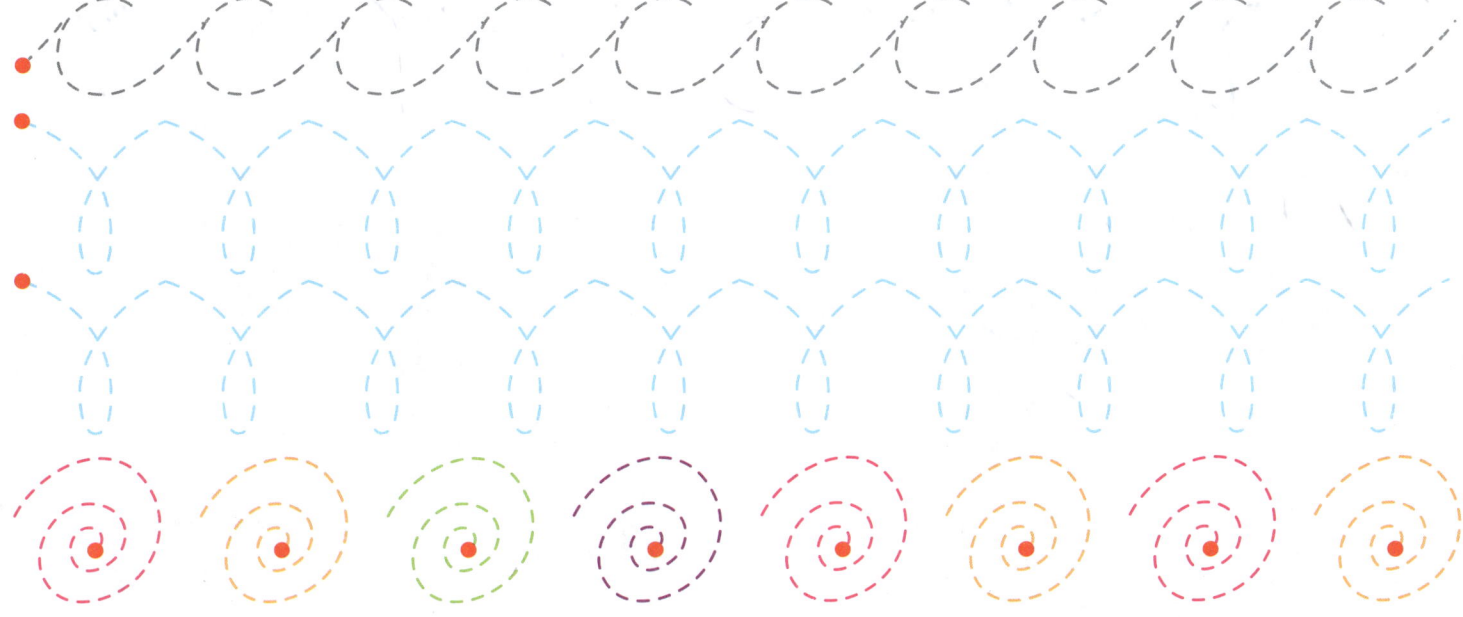

Anticlockwise—Patterns and Letters

Match the letters. One has been done for you.

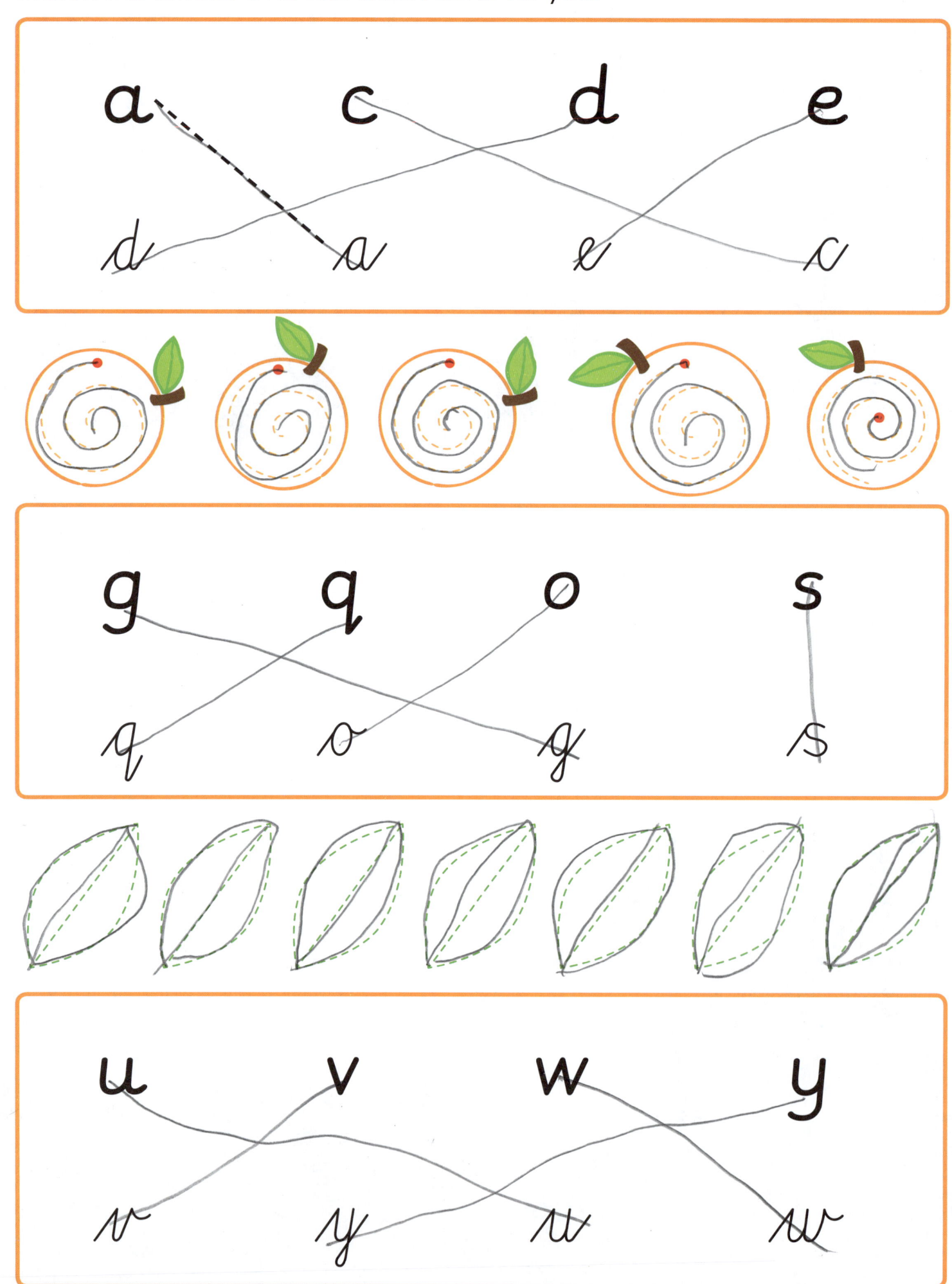

Anticlockwise—Patterns and Letters

Match the letters.

A	C	D	E
D	*a*	*E*	*C*

G	Q	O	S
Q	*g*	*S*	*O*

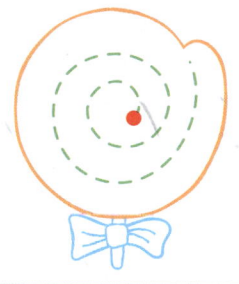   

U	V	W	Y
V	*y*	*u*	*W*

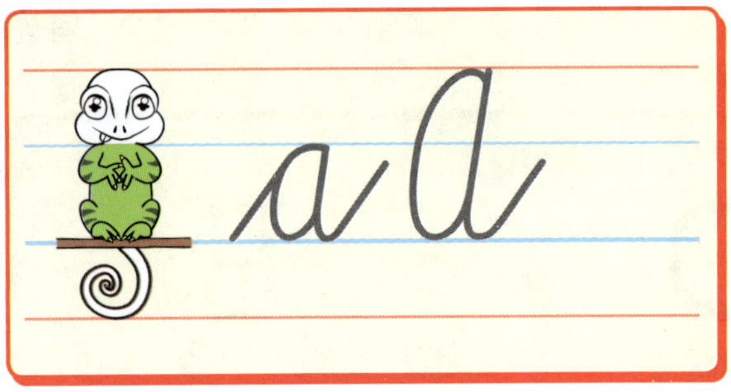

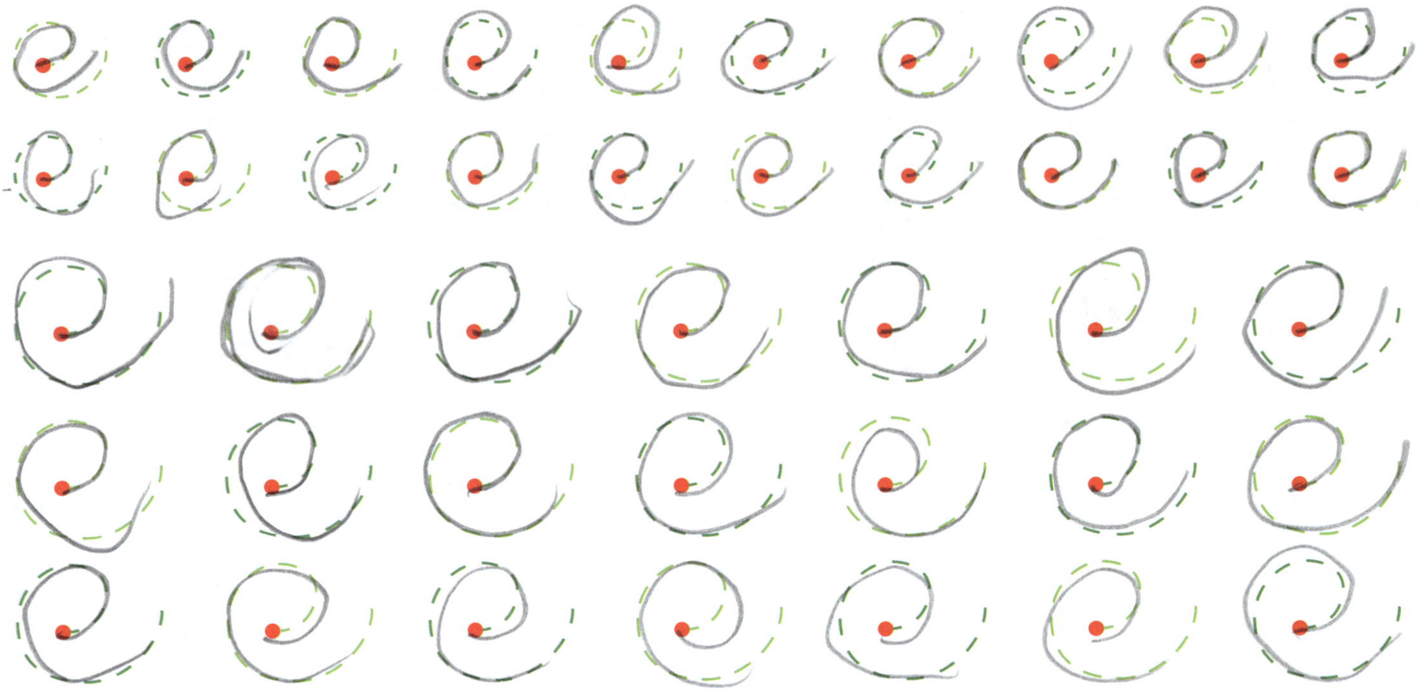

Anticlockwise Letters

Trace.

Trace.

Trace, then copy.

Trace each entry and exit stroke.

Anticlockwise Letters

a a

The exit and the entry strokes overlap to join the letters.

ant   ant

Trace, then copy.

at   am   an   and   sat   back

The man has a bat.

I have a bad cat.

Adam Ant has a big family.

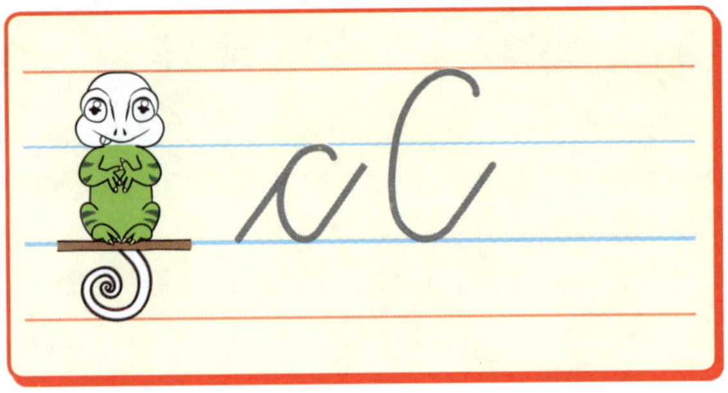

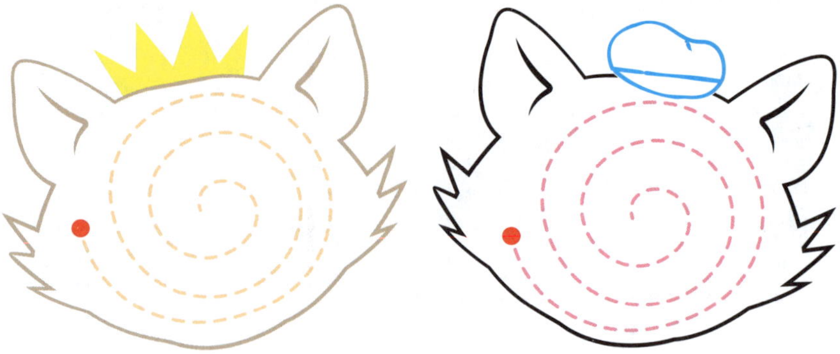

Anticlockwise Letters

cC

Trace.

Trace.

Trace, then copy.

Trace each entry and exit stroke.

Anticlockwise Letters

The exit and the entry strokes overlap to join the letters.

cap cap

Trace, then copy.

can cat cut clip kick

The clock can tick.

The cup had a crack.

Can cats creep into cars?

Anticlockwise Letters

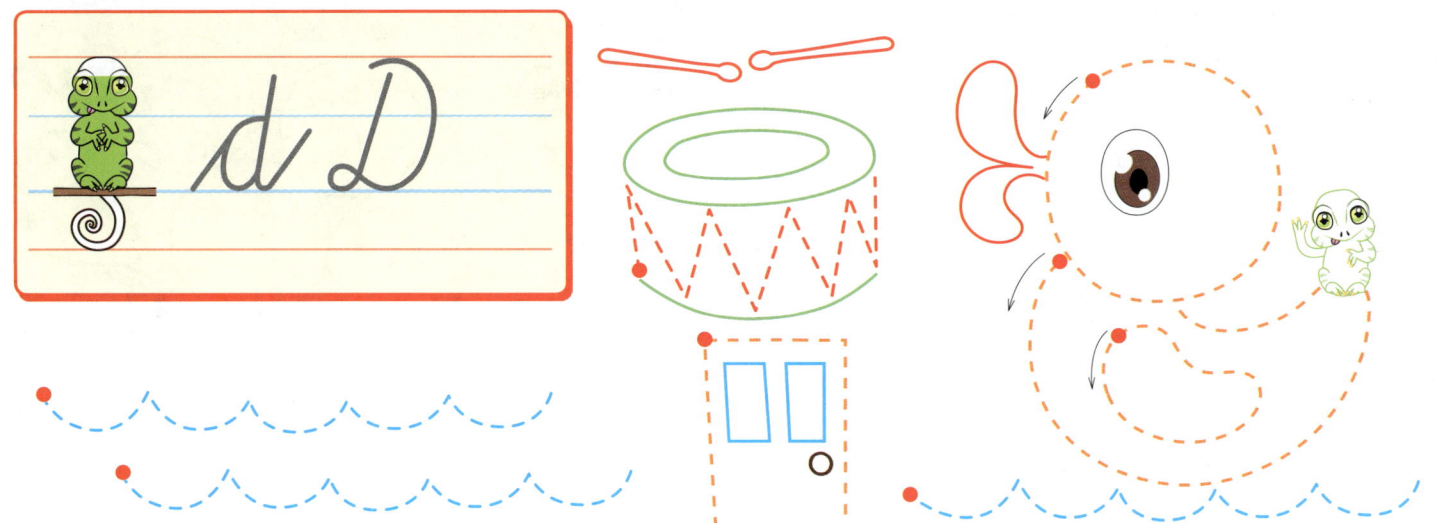

 The exit and the entry strokes overlap to join the letters.

dad dad

Trace, then copy.

dog sad duck door sand

I had a red dress.

Drop the drum at the door!

My dad had a good friend.

Anticlockwise Letters

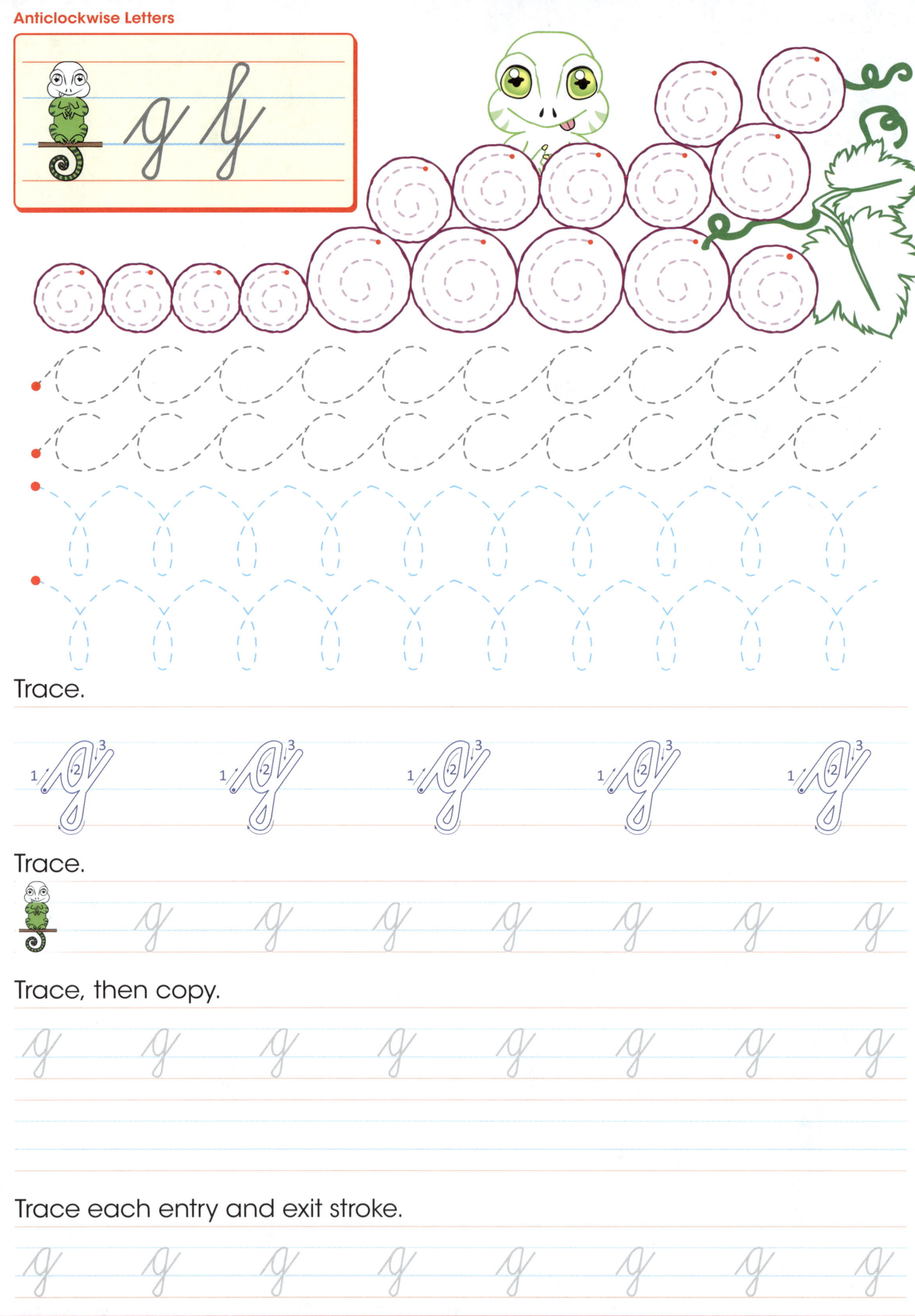

Trace.

Trace.

Trace, then copy.

Trace each entry and exit stroke.

Anticlockwise Letters

The exit and the entry strokes overlap to join the letters.

get   get

Trace, then copy.

girl big leg rug grab

The egg was good.

I am going to hug the girl.

Glue the peg to the flag.

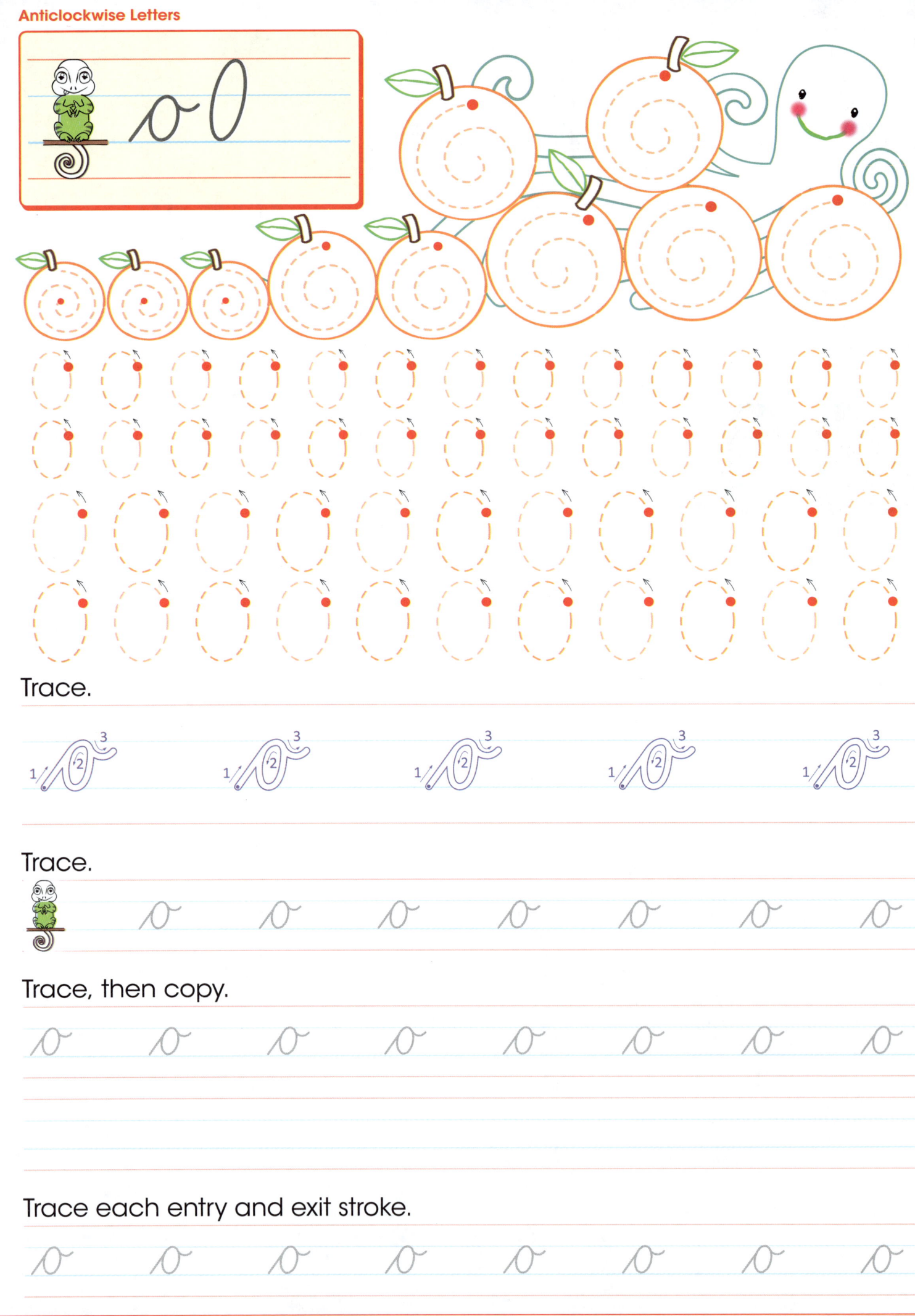

Anticlockwise Letters

The exit and the entry strokes overlap to join the letters.

on   on

Why is this join different?

Ask a friend.

Trace, then copy.

not got doll rock dog lot

Stop at the shop.

It was a long, hot day.

I cannot hop on a rock.

Anticlockwise Letters

qQ

The exit and the entry strokes overlap to join the letters.

quick quick

Trace, then copy.

quack quiz queen quiet

The queen ran quickly.

'Quack!' said the duck.

I am quiet under the quilt.

Anticlockwise Letters

e l

Trace.

Trace.

Trace, then copy.

Trace each entry and exit stroke.

Anticlockwise Letters

The exit and the entry strokes overlap to join the letters.

end   *end*

Trace, then copy.

men tent get tell help

When are you seven?

My neck is very red.

We went to see the ocean.

Anticlockwise Letters

sS

Trace.

Trace.

Trace, then copy.

Trace each entry and exit stroke.

20 NEW WAVE HANDWRITING 1ST CLASS
978-1-84654-932-8 Prim-Ed Publishing www.prim-ed.com

Anticlockwise Letters

The exit and the entry strokes overlap to join the letters.

skip   skip

Trace, then copy.

miss cross scar sleep

This mouse can skate.

She sang a silly song.

A scarf is in the house.

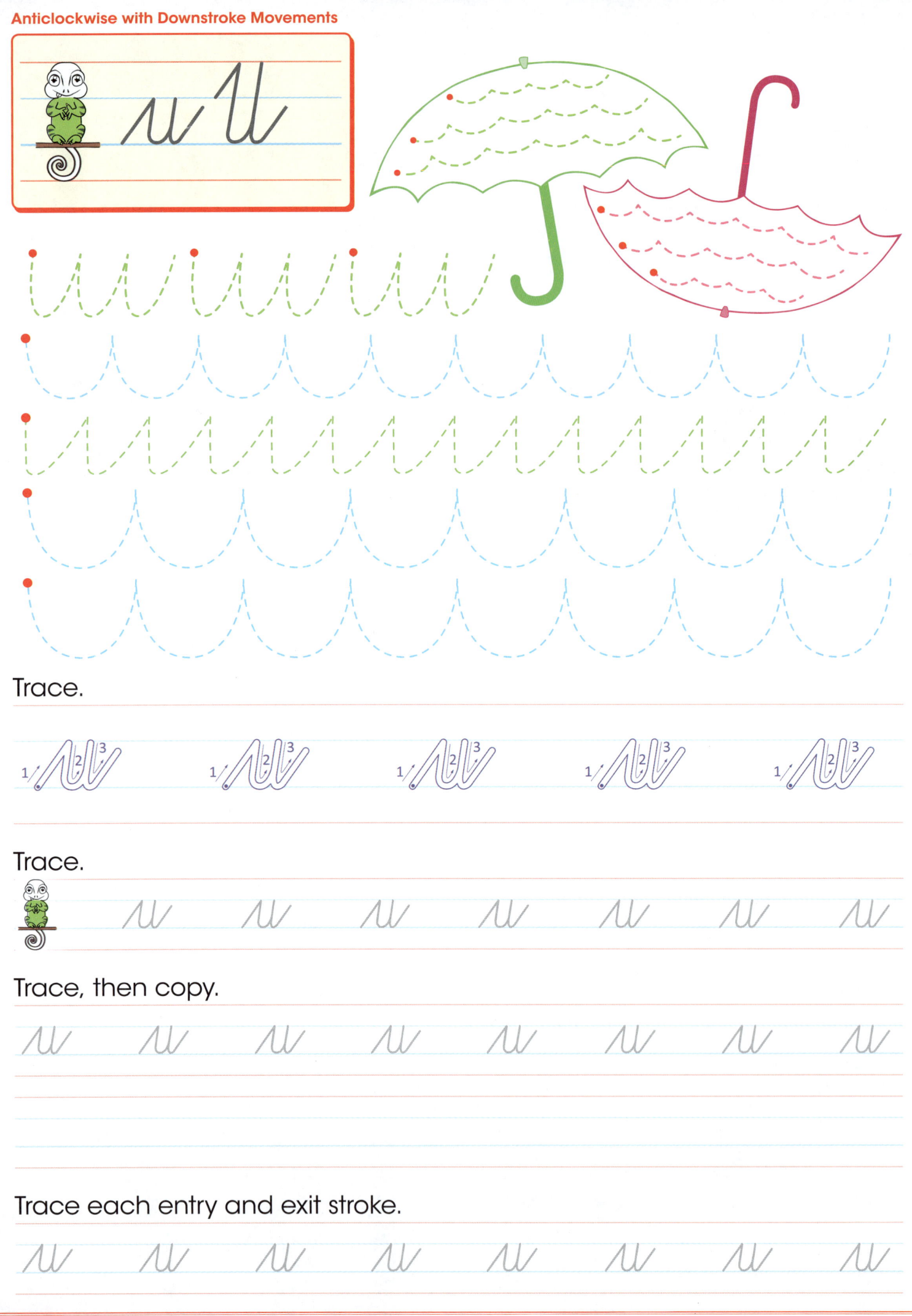

Anticlockwise with Downstroke Movements

u U

The exit and the entry strokes overlap to join the letters.

us   us

Trace, then copy.

up   but   bus   run   cup   nut

Up jumped the duck.

A drum must be fun!

Bugs run up tree trunks.

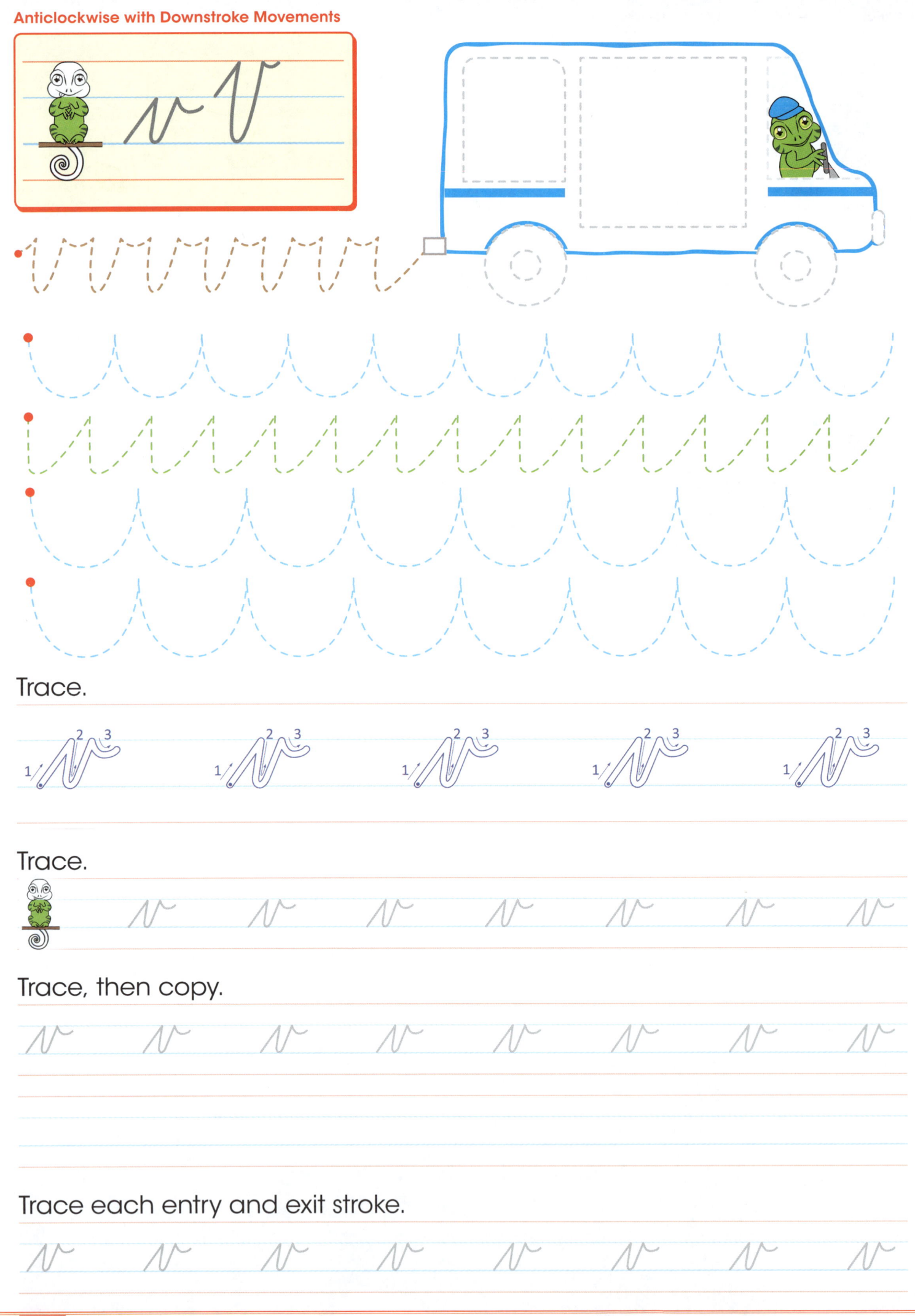

Anticlockwise with Downstroke Movements

v V

The exit and the entry strokes overlap to join the letters.

vet   vet

Why is this join different?

Ask a friend.

Trace, then copy.

vest   give   have   love   very

Five vans have arrived.

Vets are very clever.

I have eleven vests and vases.

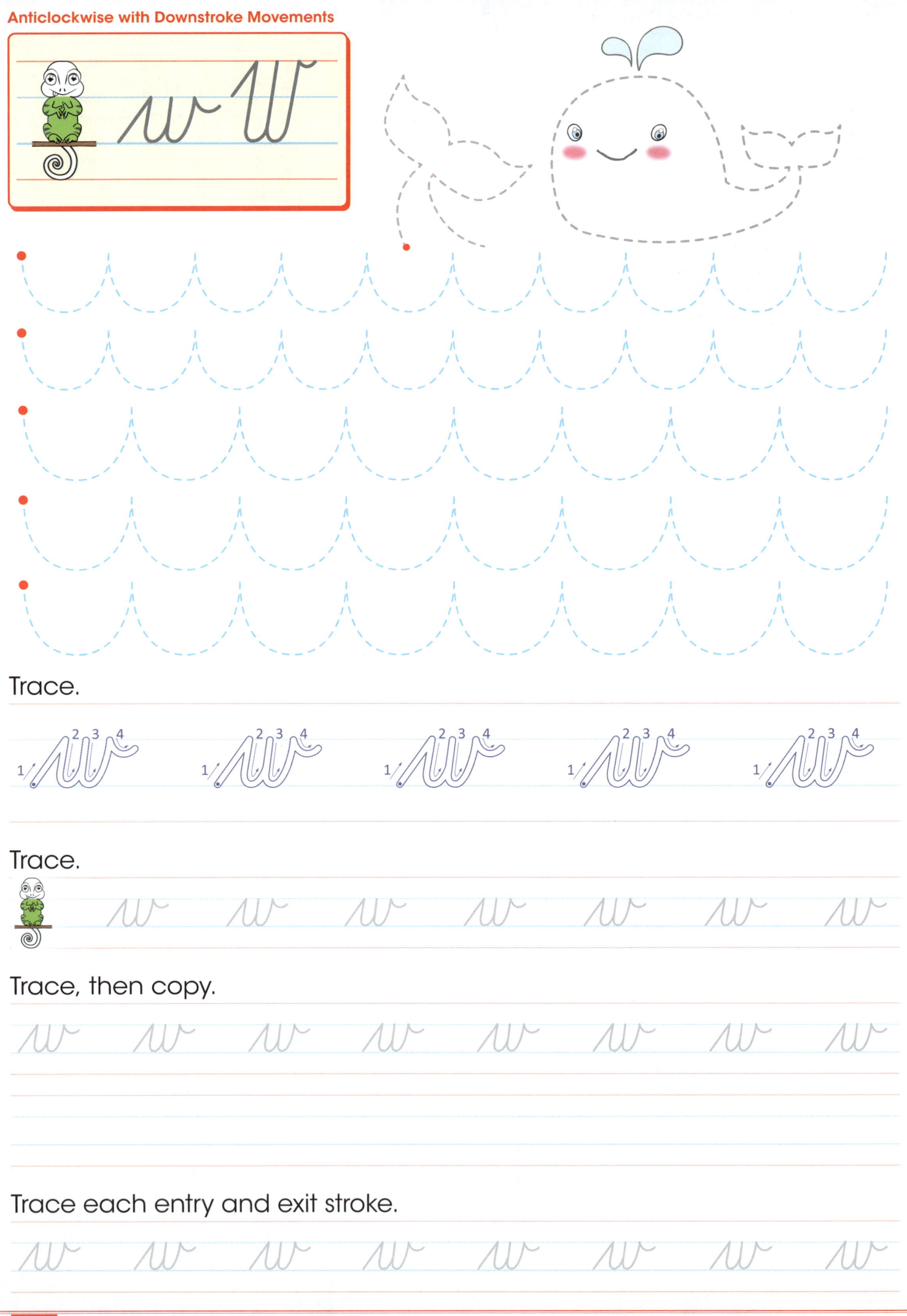

Anticlockwise with Downstroke Movements

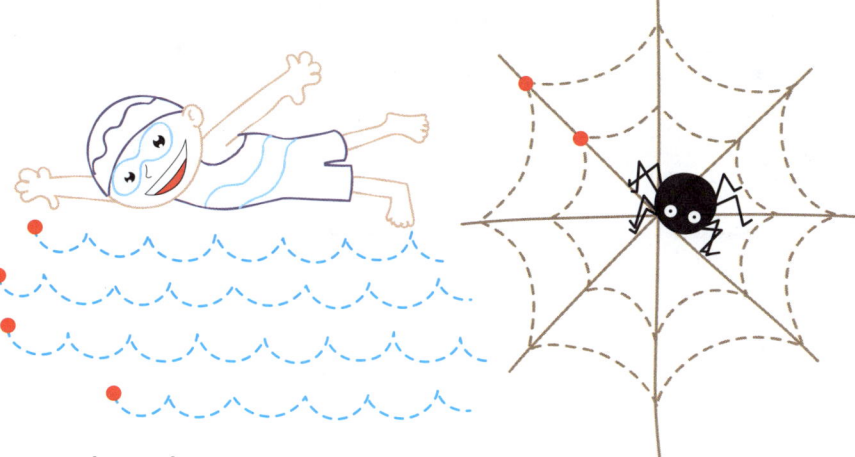

The exit and the entry strokes overlap to join the letters.

wet   *wet*

Why is this join different?

Ask a friend.

Trace, then copy.

was   what   when   twin

We swim in the water.

Why were we watching?

The twins saw a web.

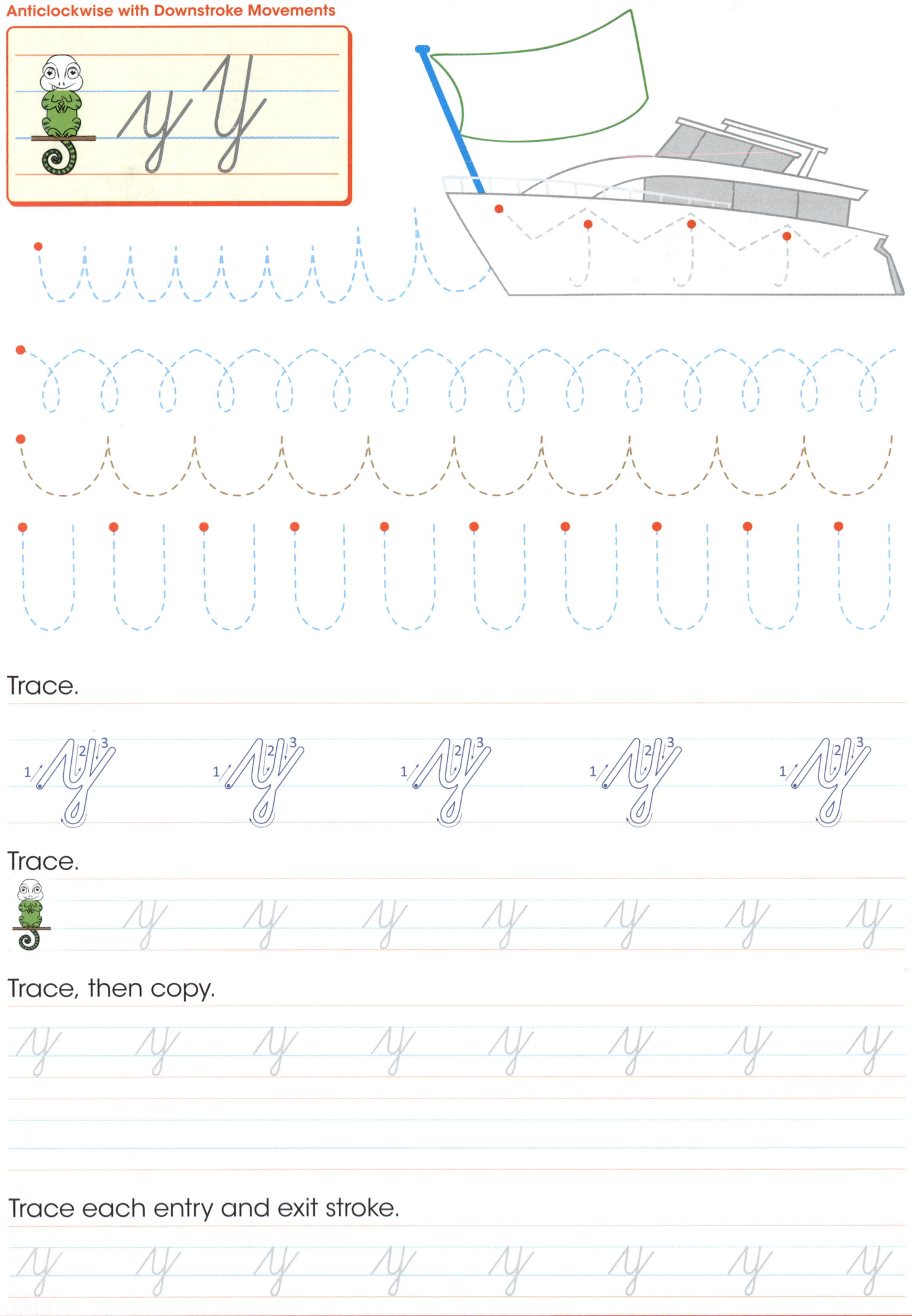

Anticlockwise with Downstroke Movements

y Y

The exit and the entry strokes overlap to join the letters.

yap   yap

Trace, then copy.

yet yes yell yawn year

Your yo-yo is yellow.

I yawn in my yard.

I like egg yolks and yoghurt.

Revision—Anticlockwise

Trace the letters.

a c o e s u v w

g q y

d

A C O E S U V W

Q D

G Y

Read, trace, then copy the words.

back   cannot   yelled   you

house   twelve   grin   quail

Revision—Anticlockwise

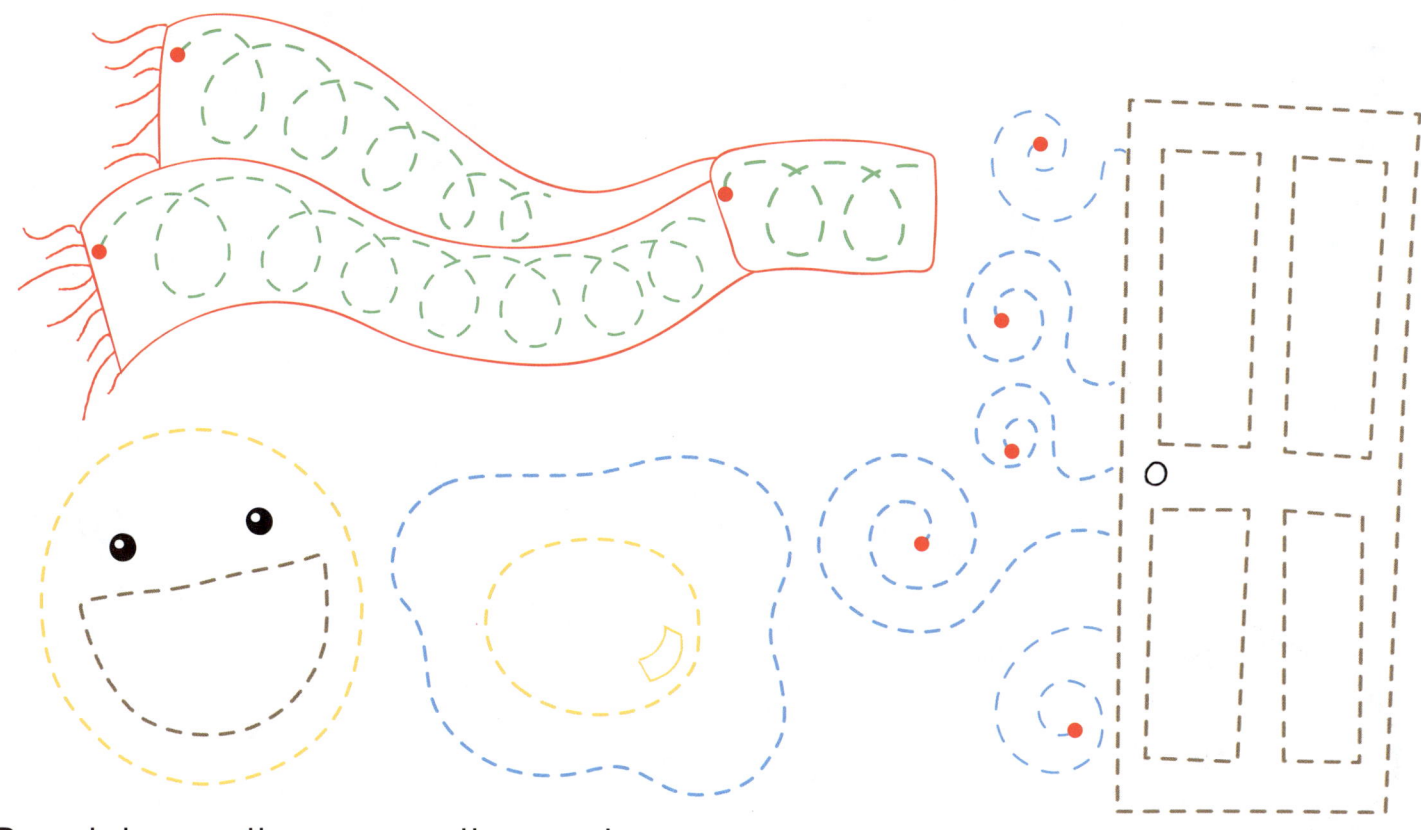

Read, trace, then copy the sentences.

We are glad we went.

Give the scarf to me!

Shut the door quickly!

Use twelve good egg yolks.

Clockwise—Patterns and Letters

Match the letters.

z   x   Z   X

𝓍   𝓏   𝒳   𝒵

Clockwise Letter

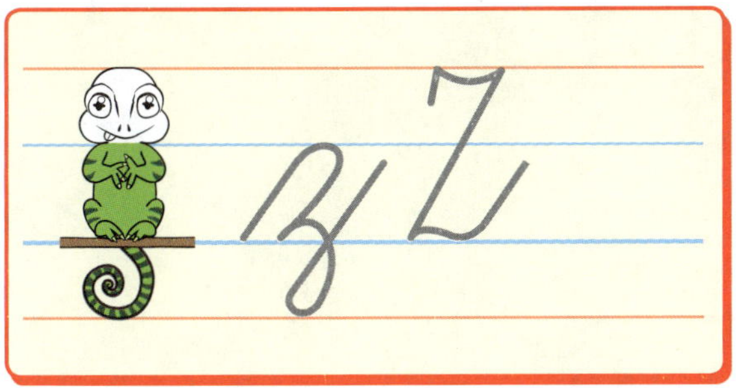

z Z

Trace.

Trace.

Trace, then copy.

Trace each entry and exit stroke.

Clockwise Letter

zZ

The exit and the entry strokes overlap to join the letters.

zoo   zoo

Trace, then copy.

zip zero zebra zoom zap

Zack did a quiz.

He won a prize.

Bees buzz but drinks fizz.

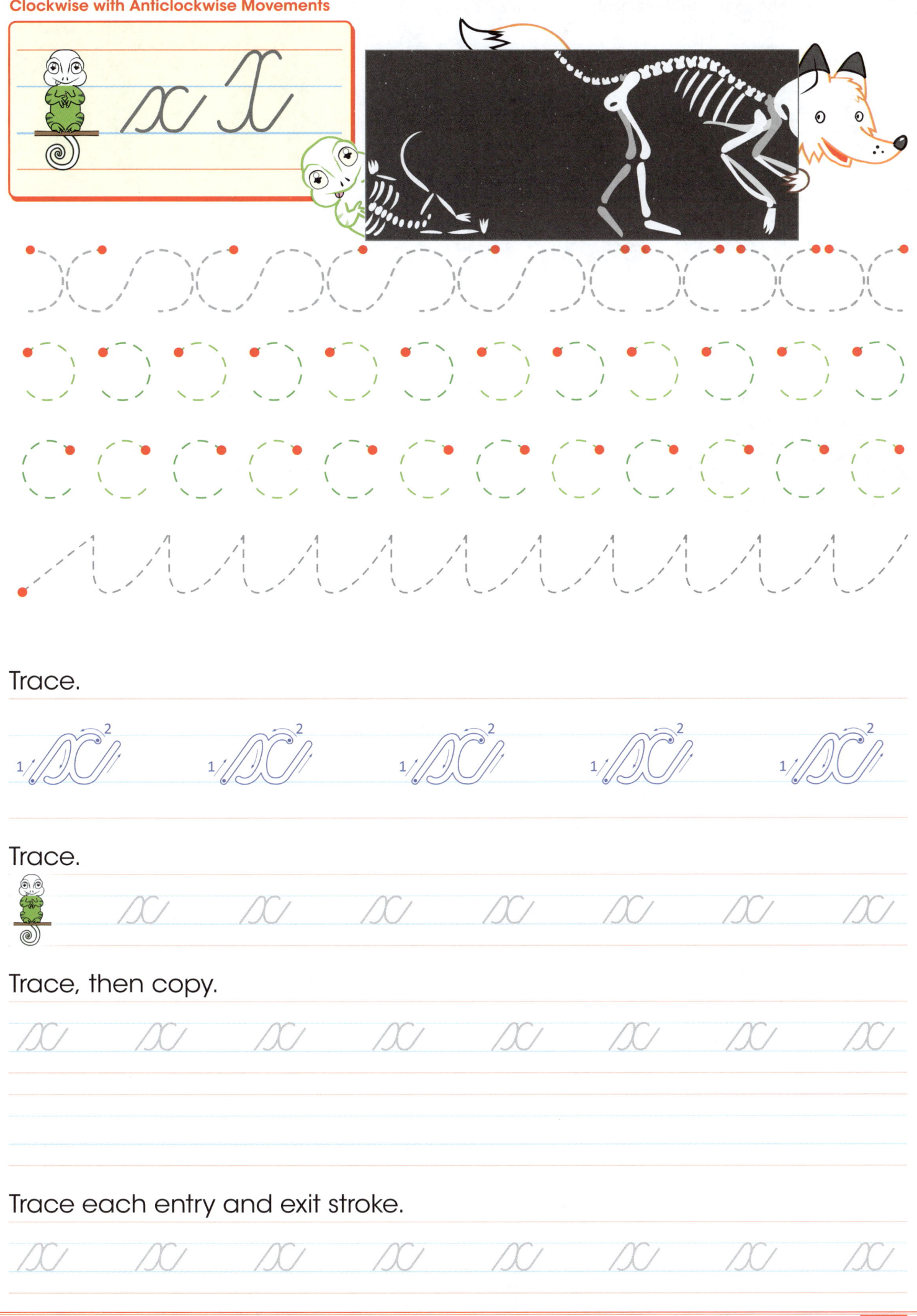

Clockwise with Anticlockwise Movements

xX

The exit and the entry strokes overlap to join the letters.

boxes   boxes

Trace, then copy.

six fox mix next exact

She fixed the six boxes.

He was very excited.

My birthday is next week.

Revision—Clockwise

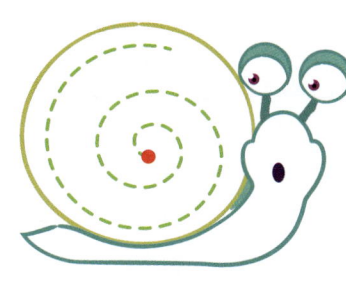

Trace and copy the letters.

 *x*

 *z*

 *X*

Z

Read, trace, then copy the words.

puzzle buzz axe ox

Read, trace, then copy the sentences.

Mazes are exciting for foxes.

Don't sneeze on the cake mix.

Downstroke—Patterns and Letters

Match the letters.

i	l	j	t
j	t	i	l

m	n	p	r	h	k
n	m	r	h	p	k

b	f
f	b

Downstroke—Patterns and Letters

Match the letters.

I	L	J	T
𝒥	𝒥	𝒥	ℒ

M	N	P	R	H	K
𝓃	𝓂	ℛ	ℋ	𝓅	𝒦

B	F
ℱ	ℬ

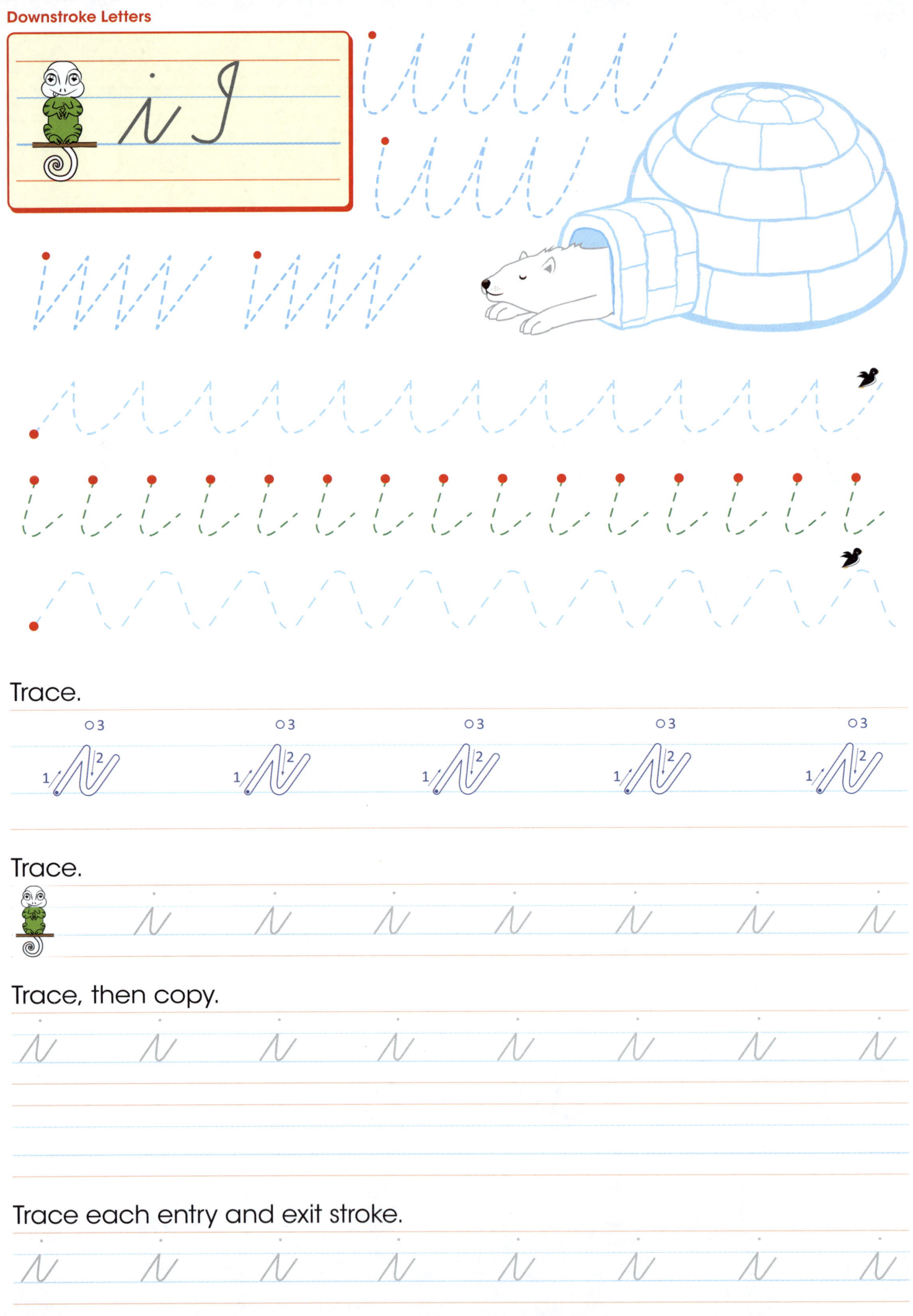

Downstroke Letters

The exit and the entry strokes overlap to join the letters.

Trace, then copy.

it in did his win ink

Will this fish sing?

I live on a little ship.

I am in the big igloo.

Downstroke Letters

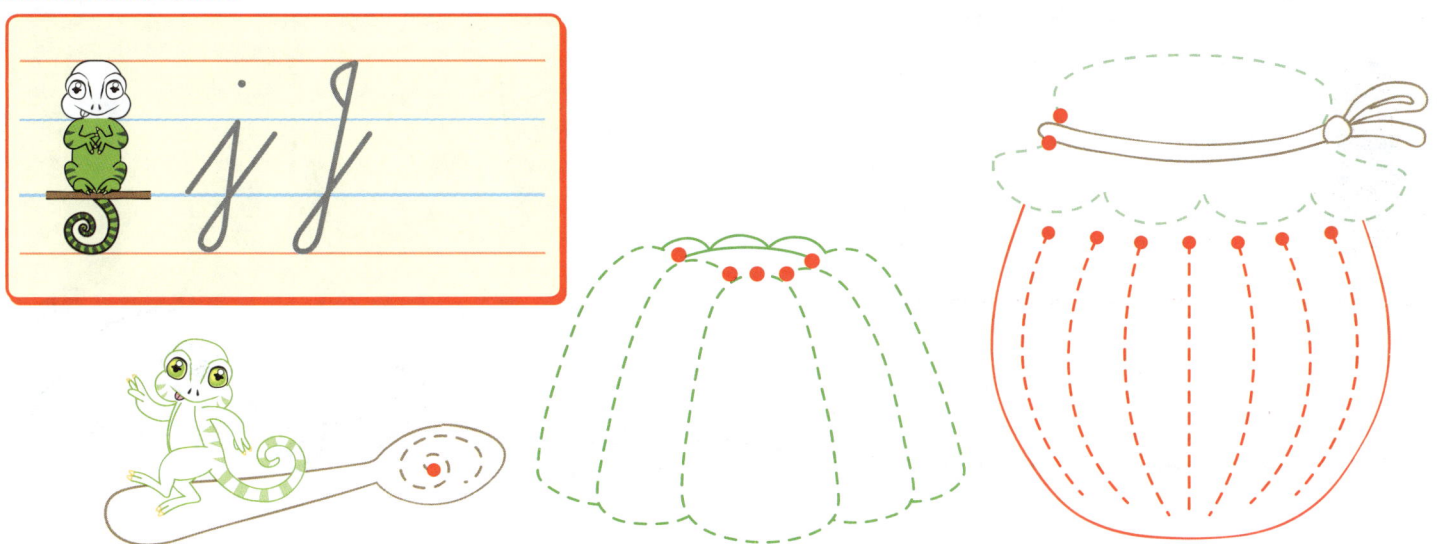

The exit and the entry strokes overlap to join the letters.

jump   jump

Trace, then copy.

jam   jug   job   just   jet

I enjoy eating jelly.

Jump in the jungle.

Jellyfish juggle jelly beans.

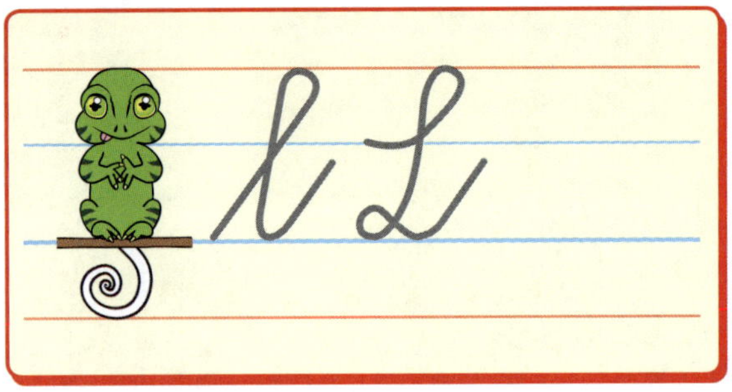

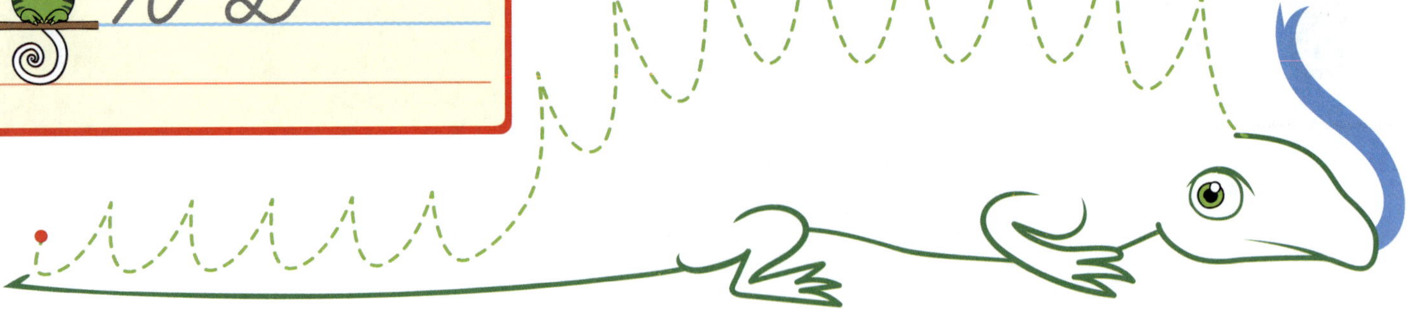

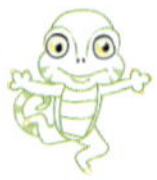

Downstroke Letters

ℓ L

Trace.

Trace.

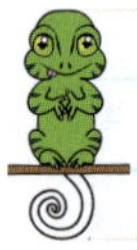

Trace, then copy.

Trace each entry and exit stroke.

Downstroke Letters

The exit and the entry strokes overlap to join the letters.

leaf *leaf*

Trace, then copy.

look well help ball cliff

I like cold milk.

The quilt will be soft.

Look at the blue ball.

Downstroke Letters

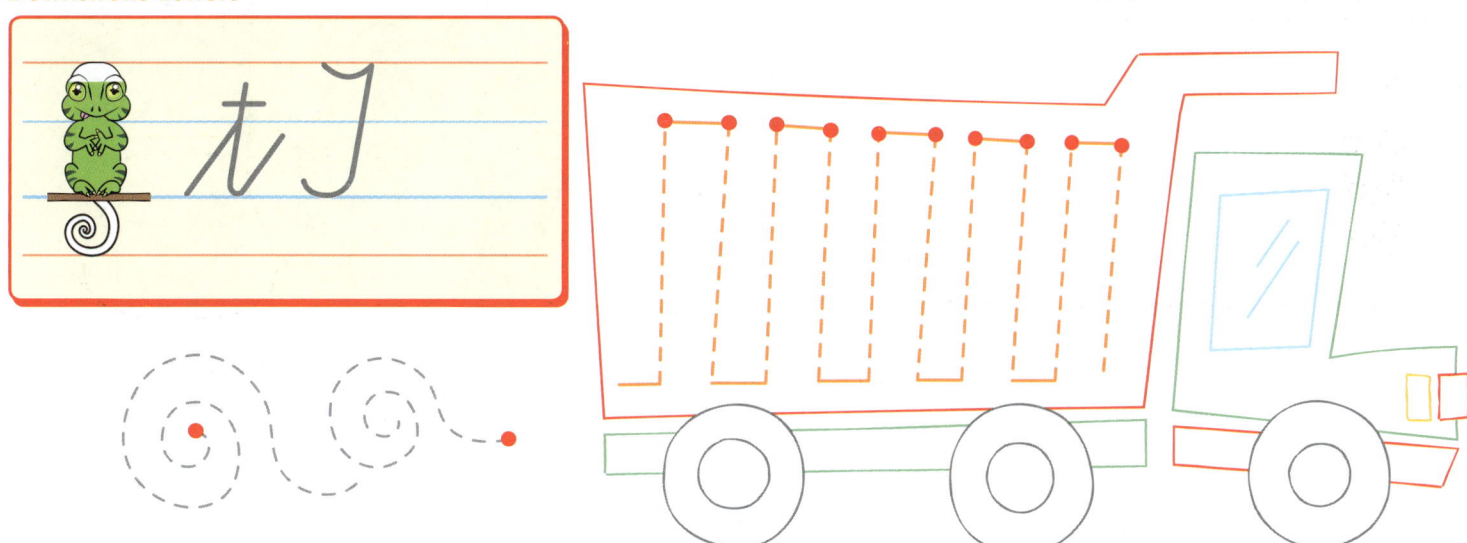

The exit and the entry strokes overlap to join the letters.

tree tree

Trace, then copy.

try tent trap want twist

My best truck is bent.

The little boy was lost.

It is better to start last.

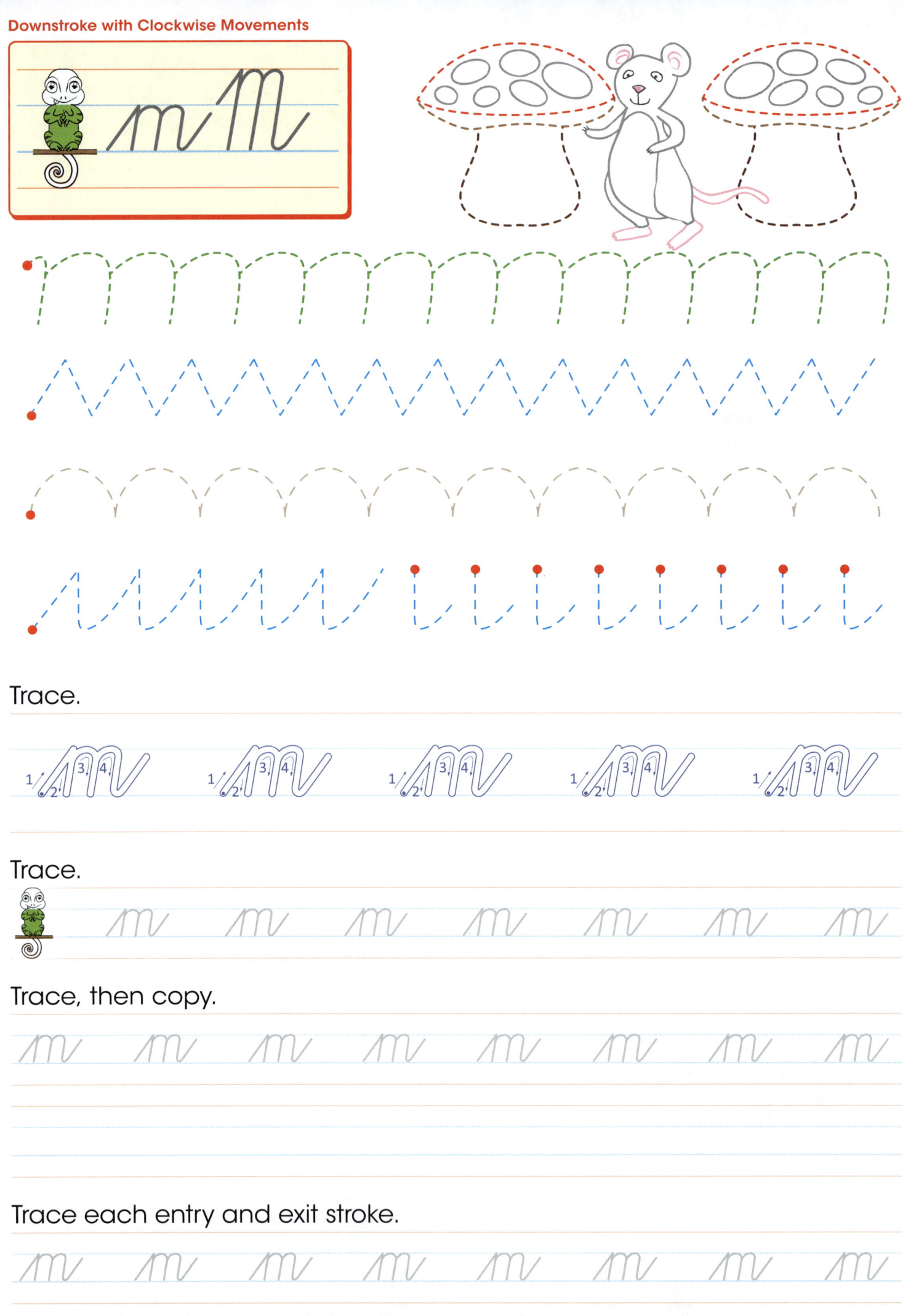

Downstroke with Clockwise Movements

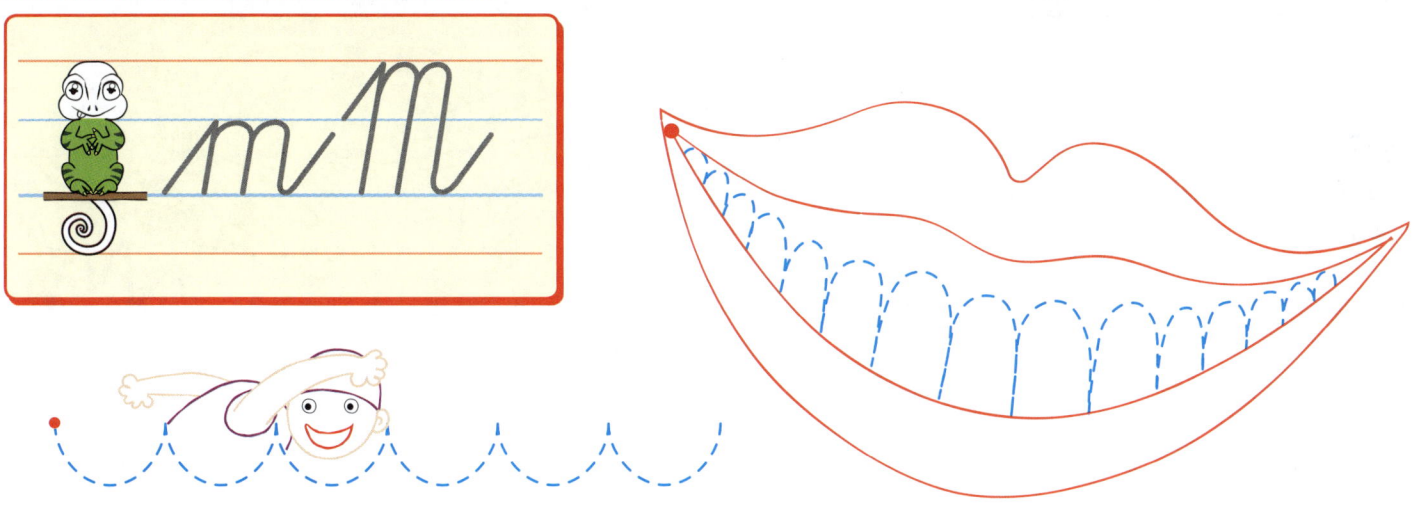

The exit and the entry strokes overlap to join the letters.

men   men

Trace, then copy.

made   man   camp   smell

Mum hummed a song.

He made a small smile.

Swimming is fun in summer.

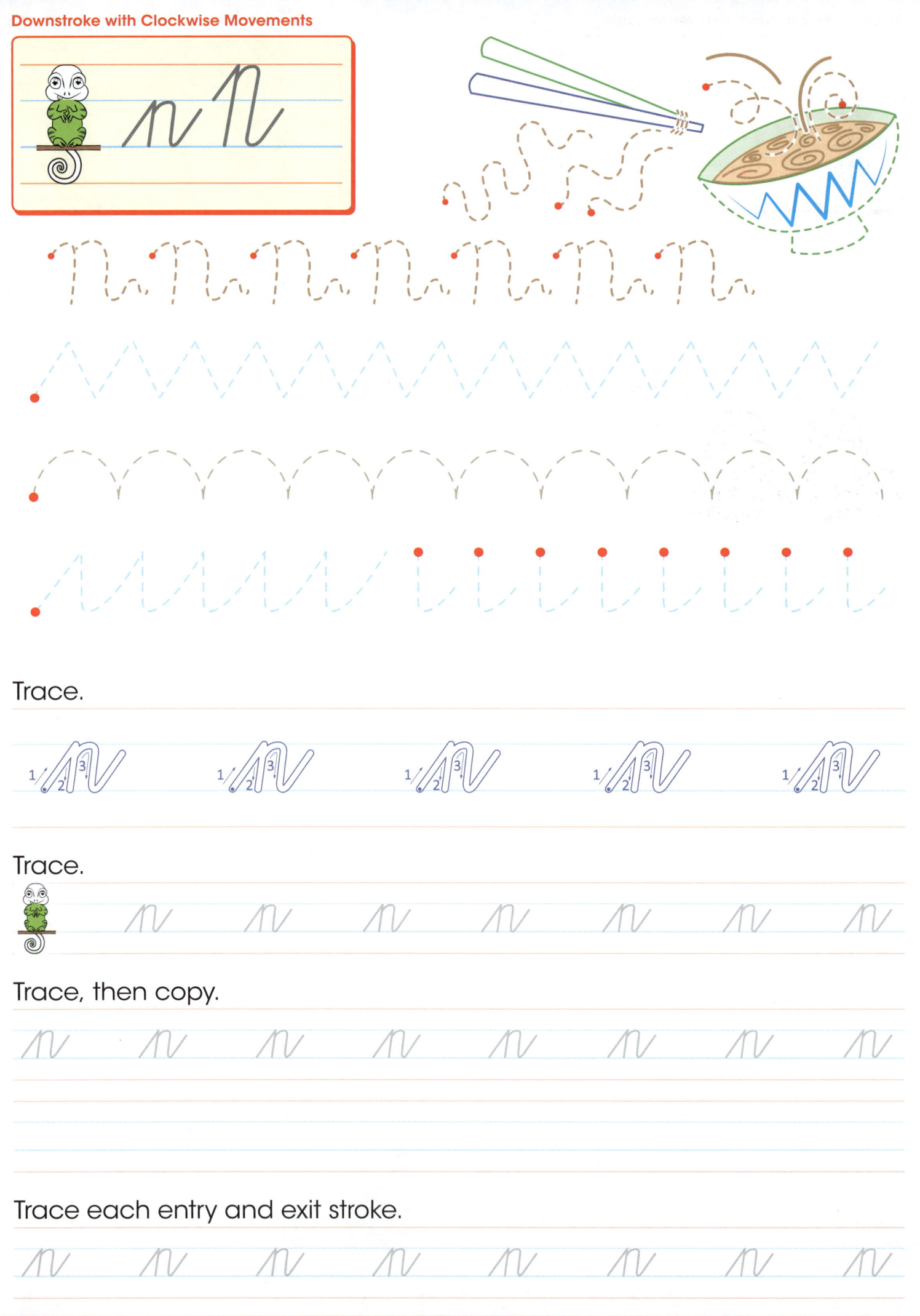

Downstroke with Clockwise Movements

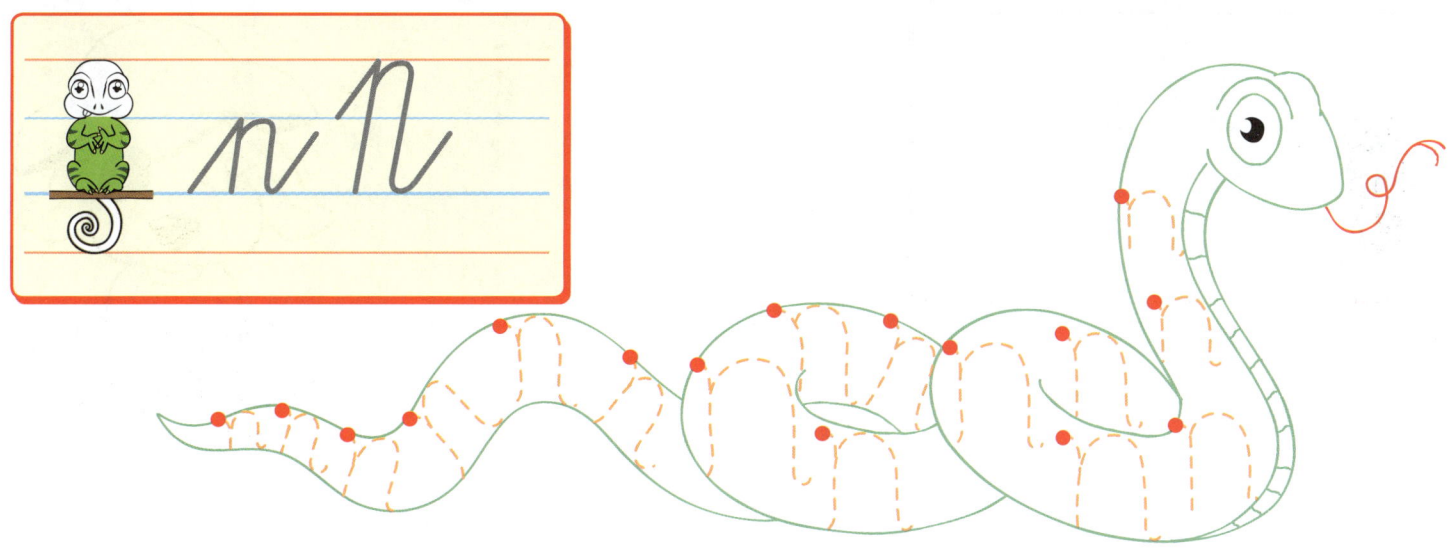

The exit and the entry strokes overlap to join the letters.

net   net

Trace, then copy.

sun   can   snack   snap   nine

Snakes snack in the sun.

Dinner is on the table.

I cannot snip the long ribbon.

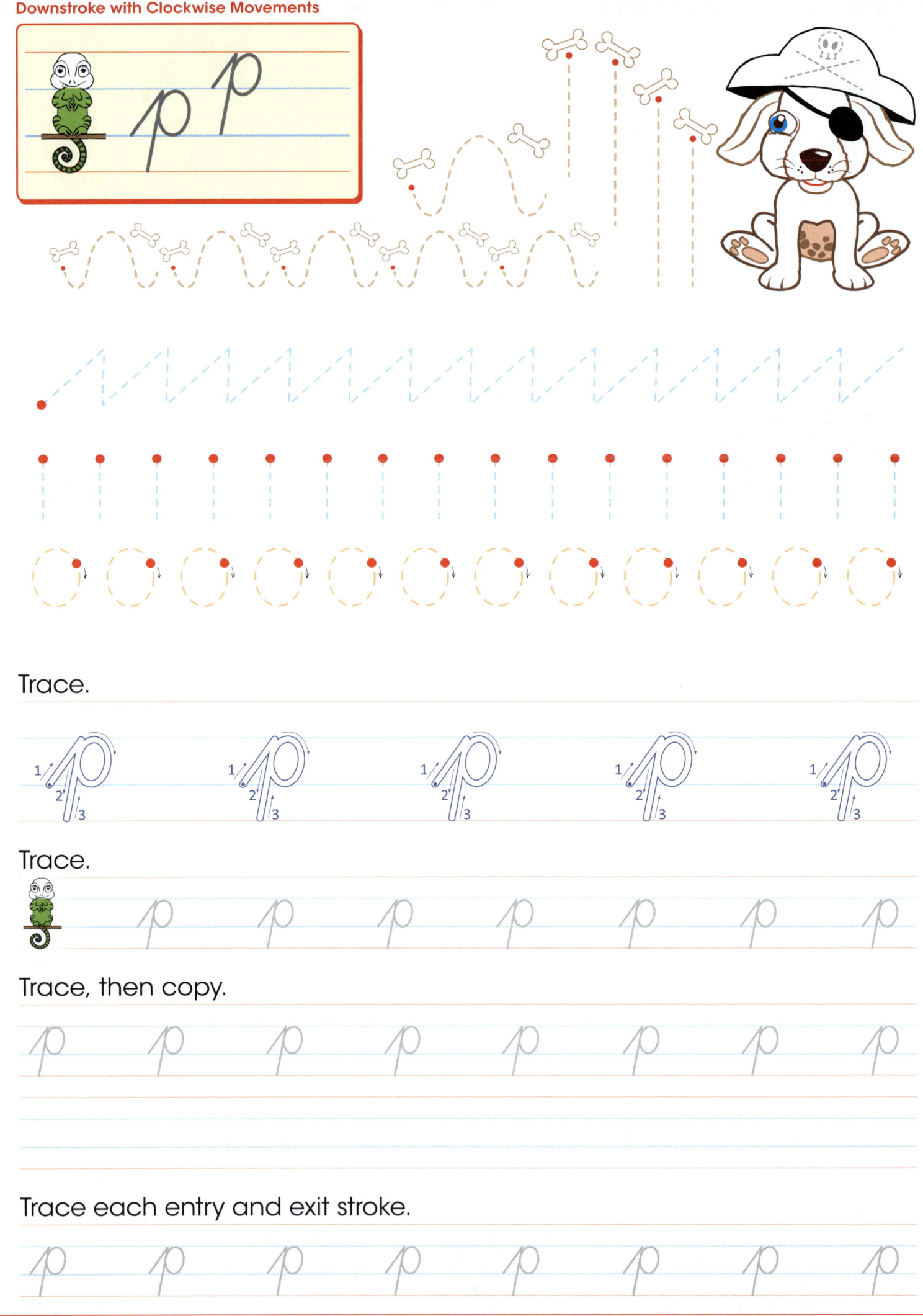

Downstroke with Clockwise Movements

p p

The exit and the entry strokes overlap to join the letters.

pig   pig

Trace, then copy.

pram   plane   puppy   kept

Push the pram up the hill.

I plan to speak to him.

Do not spill a drop.

Downstroke with Clockwise Movements

rR

Trace.

Trace.

Trace, then copy.

Trace each entry and exit stroke.

54 NEW WAVE HANDWRITING **1ST CLASS**

Downstroke with Clockwise Movements

rR

The exit and the entry strokes overlap to join the letters.

rock   rock

Why is this join different?

Ask a friend.

Trace, then copy.

ring   read   rake   rode   ran

I ride my bike very well.

Ron can carry the rock.

She read her bird book.

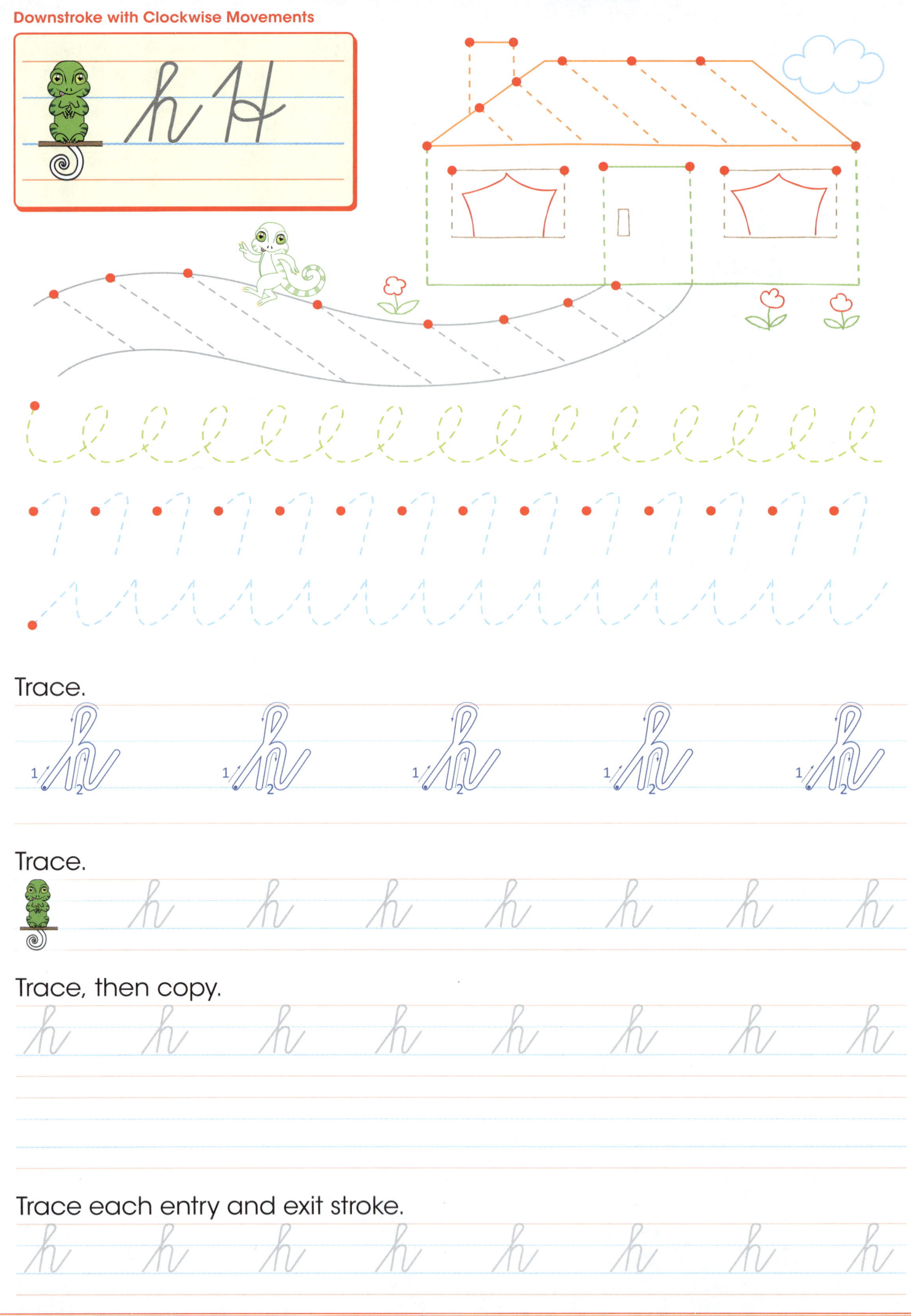

Downstroke with Clockwise Movements

h H

The exit and the entry strokes overlap to join the letters.

house house

Trace, then copy.

him hit hill home hope

He has a home here.

The house is on a hill.

We are having hot cheese.

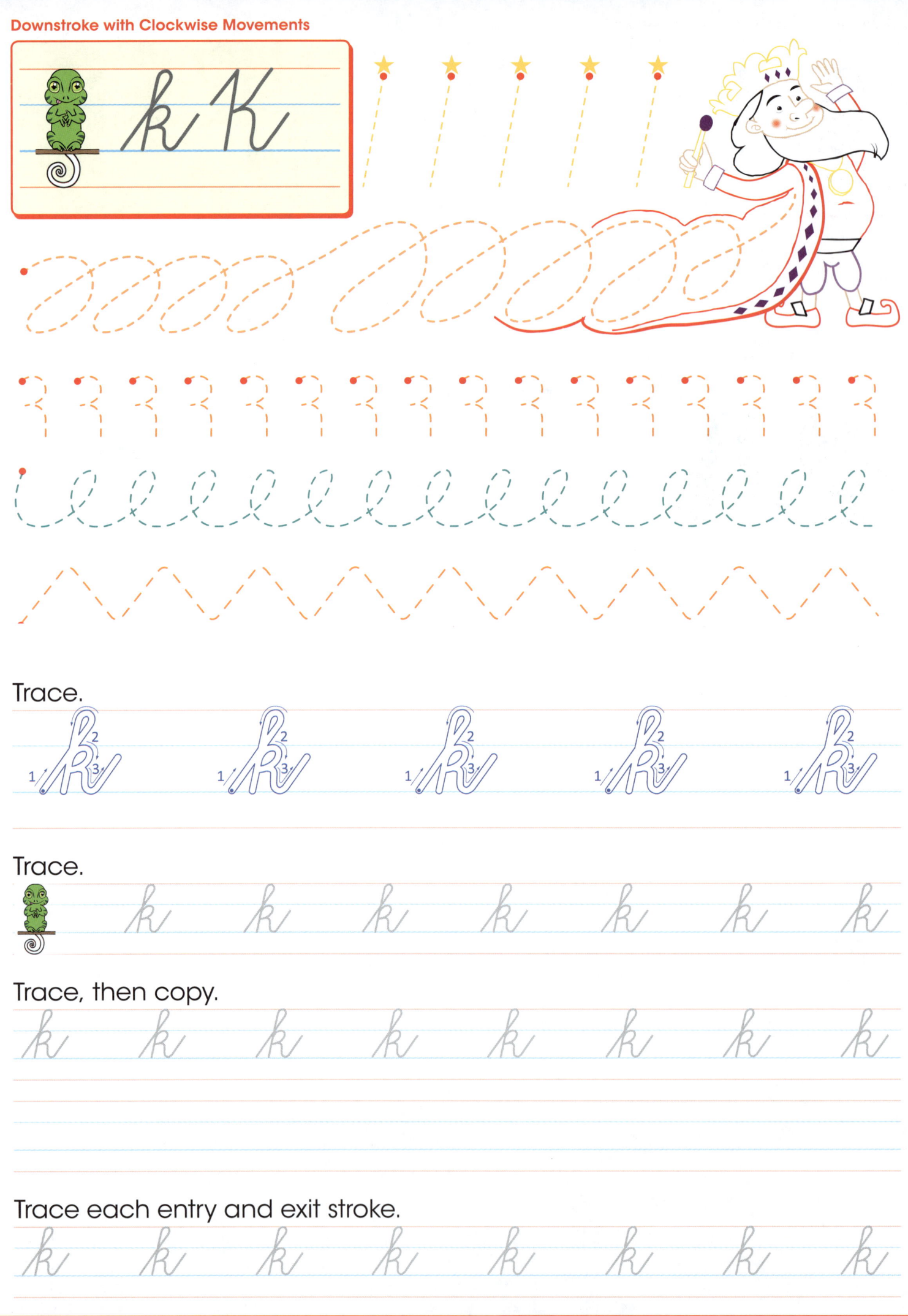

Downstroke with Clockwise Movements

k K

The exit and the entry strokes overlap to join the letters.

king king

Trace, then copy.

kiss kick clock quack

The kitten runs quickly.

King Karl likes to kiss.

Kick the black brick! Ouch!

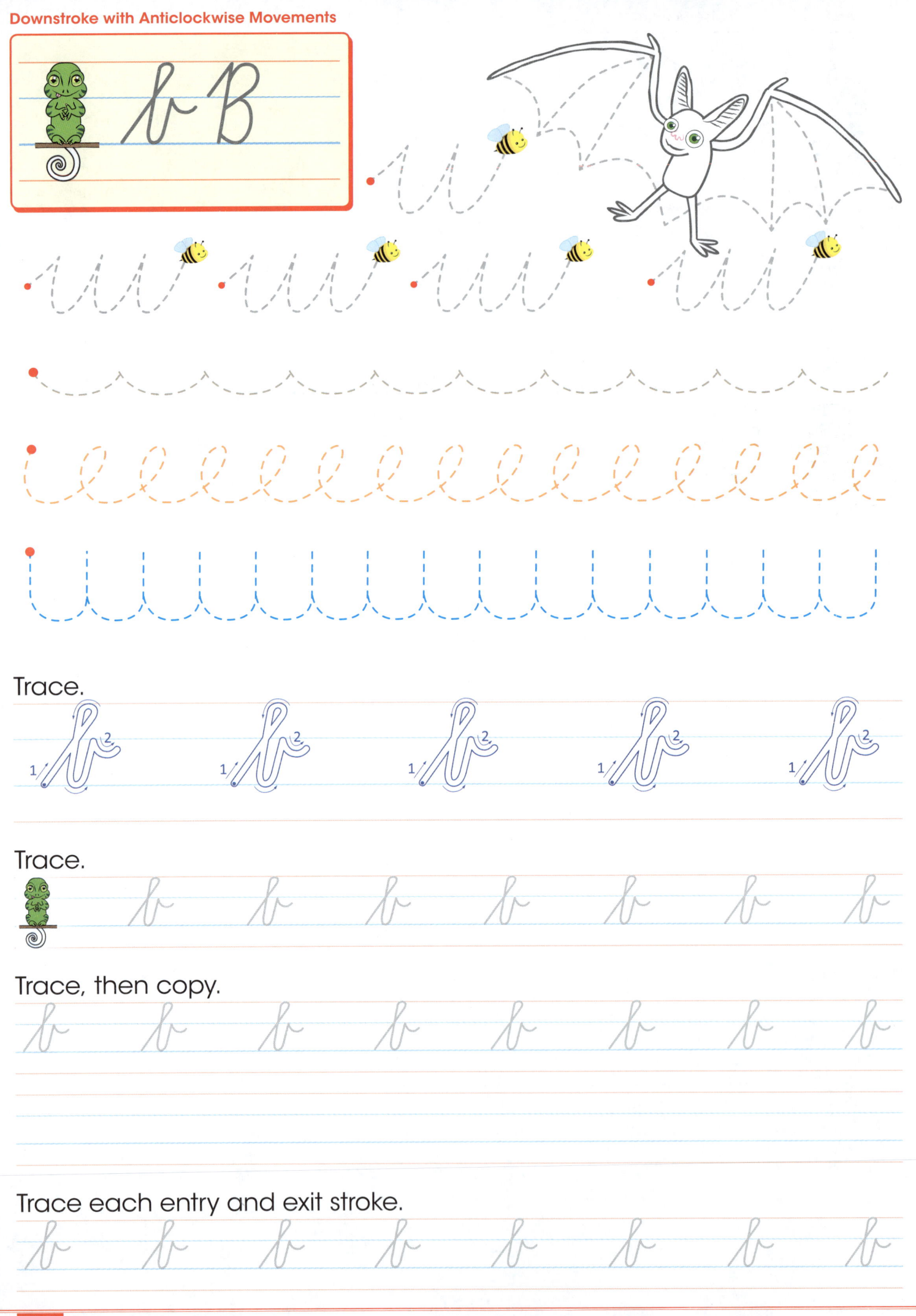

Downstroke with Anticlockwise Movements

b B

The exit and the entry strokes overlap to join the letters.

bat bat

Why is this join different?

Ask a friend.

Trace, then copy.

bar bug bell big bed bag

The block is big and blue.

Bring back the black ball!

The rabbit bit the balloon.

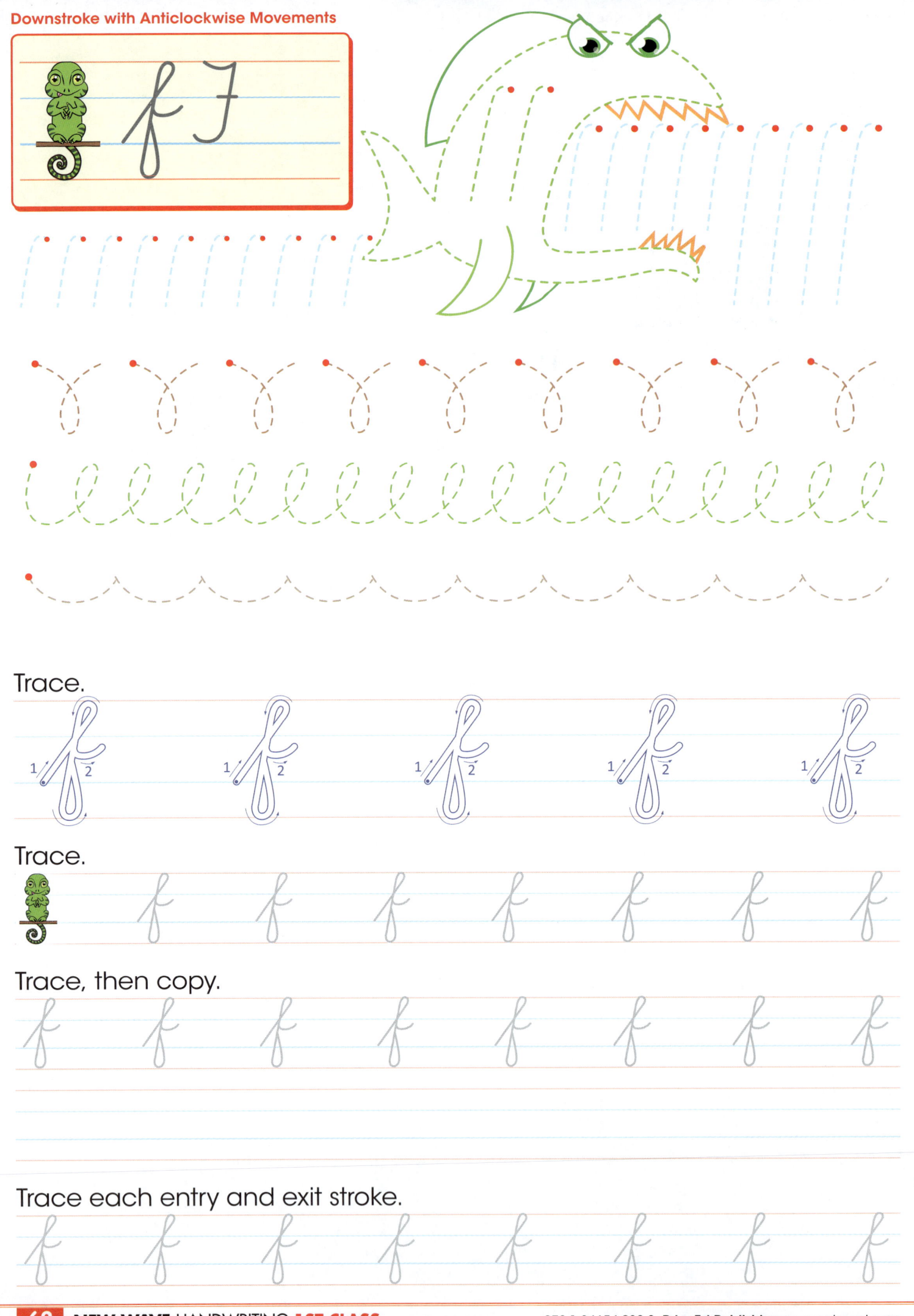

Downstroke with Anticlockwise Movements

f F

The exit and the entry strokes overlap to join the letters.

fog   fog

Why is this join different?

Ask a friend.

Trace, then copy.

if off fat fog fun foot

Fred Frog fell off the leaf.

The flag is flat and soft.

Five fish float and feed.

Revision—Downstroke

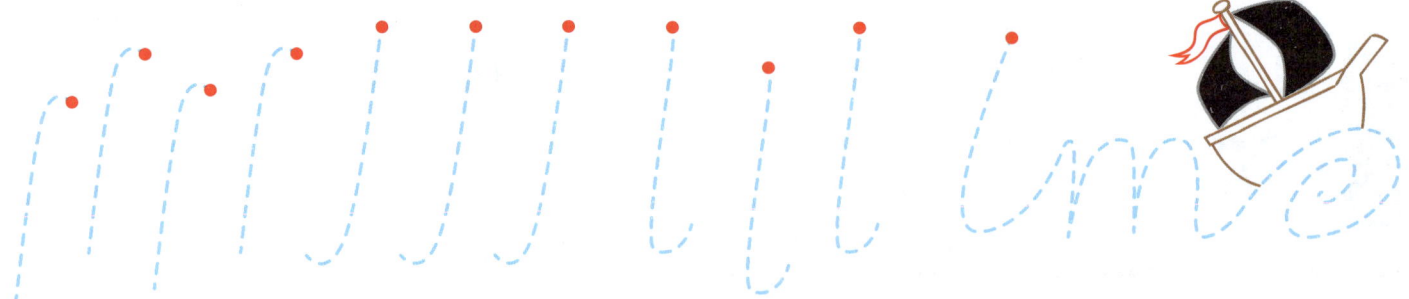

Trace the letters.

i m n r

j p

l h k b t

f

J M N R P

L J H K B F

J

Read, trace, then copy the words.

pick fill pump snack if

bit rub here start little

Revision—Downstroke

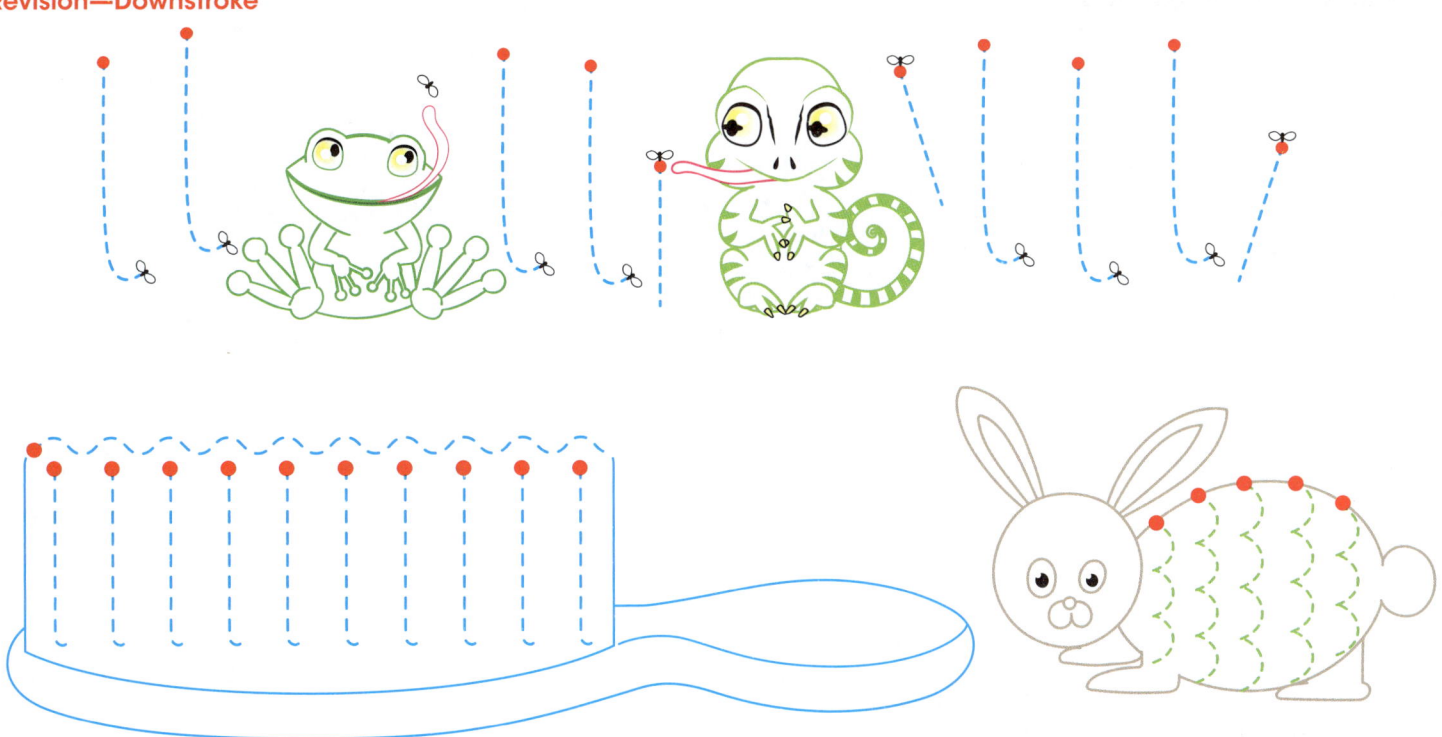

Read, trace, then copy the sentences.

My jacket feels soft.

She kicked the ball.

Rabbits cannot swim.

Last night was funny.

Revision—Lower-case Letters

Trace, then copy each letter.

Using Capital Letters

All capital letters except *P, O, V* and *W* join to the next letter.

Trace and copy using joined capital letters.

April   Barry

Cathy   December

Eamonn   February

Gail   Harry

Ireland   July

Kerry   Lara

Using Capital Letters

Trace and copy using joined capital letters.

Monday

November

Quinn

Reagan

September

Tuesday

Upton

Xavier

Yale

Zaan

> Remember, capital letters *P*, *O*, *V* and *W* don't join to the next letter.

Trace using unjoined capital letters.

Victoria

Wednesday

October

Patrick

Revision—Letters

1. Sort the alphabet letters into the correct boxes.
2. Check that you have included all the letters.

Pangram

Trace the sentence.

The quick brown fox jumps over the lazy dog.

Copy the sentence.

Circle a face to rate your writing.

1. Did you form your letters correctly?

2. Do your letters sit in the correct lines?

3. Did you include a capital letter and a full stop?

4. How do you rate your writing overall?

Trace, then complete the sentences. Put a full stop at the end.

My favourite food is

Outside, I like to play

Inside, I like to play

I like to learn

I am a good

Cross-curricular—Science

Label the main features of the lizard.

Trace the sentences.

Lizards have eyes.
Lizards have a nose.
Lizards have a mouth.
Lizards have a body.
Lizards have a long tongue.
They use it to find insects.

Cross-curricular—Mathematics

Trace, then copy the two-dimensional shape names.

 *circle*

 *square*

 *rectangle*

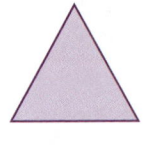 *triangle*

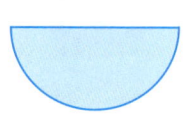 *semicircle*

Tick the shapes above with four sides.

Circle the shapes above with curved sides.

Trace, then copy the three-dimensional shape names.

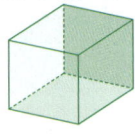 *cube*

 *cuboid*

 *cylinder*

 *sphere*

Cross-curricular—History

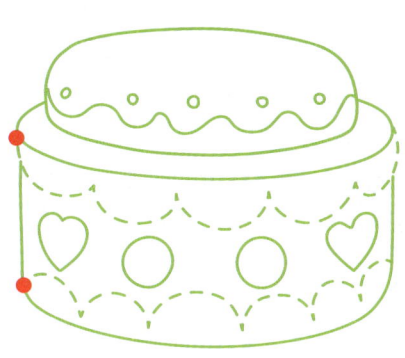

Read, trace, then complete the sentences.

When I was one,

I could not run.

When I was four,

I could open the door.

Complete the sentence, then draw candles on the last cake above.

Now I am _____, *I can*

Cross-curricular—Social, Personal and Health Education

Trace, then copy these healthy lunchbox ideas.

I can pack fresh fruit.

I can pack popcorn.

I can pack vegetable sticks.

I can pack water.

I can pack a sandwich.

Cross-curricular—Geography

Spring   Summer   Autumn   Winter

Read, trace, then copy the sentences.

In summer, I wear cool

clothing. It is hot.

In winter, I wear warm

clothing. It is cold.

Complete the sentence.

The season I like best is

Cross-curricular—Physical Education

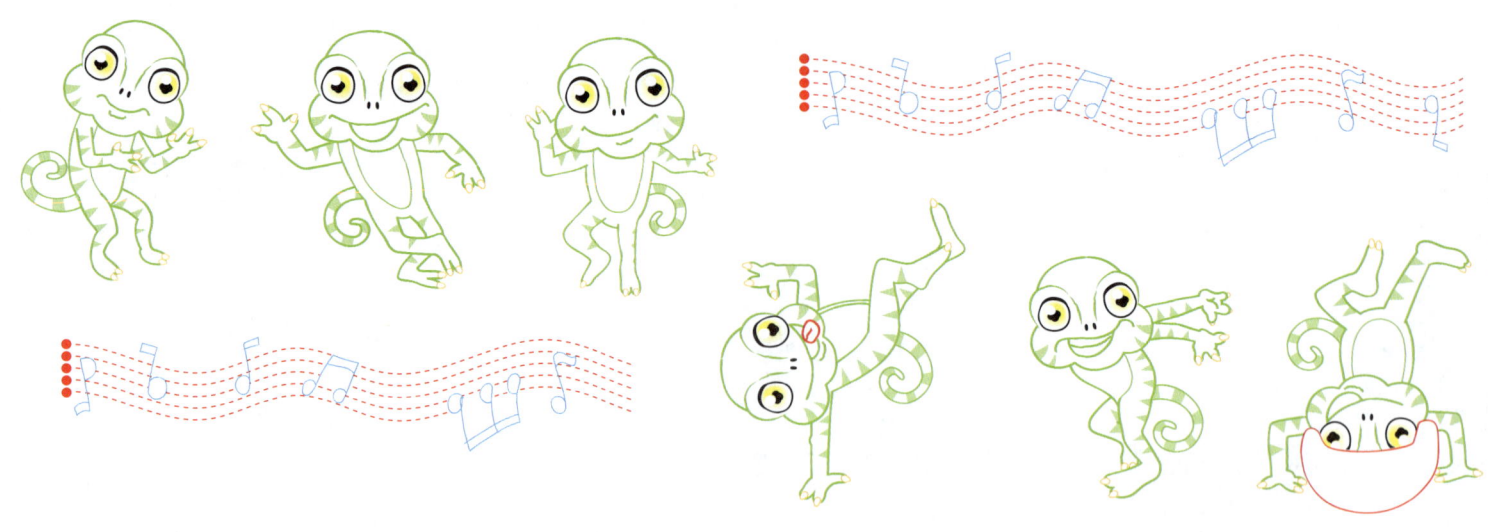

Read, trace, then copy the sentences.

When the music is fast, you

have to dance quickly.

When the music is slow, you

have to dance slowly.

Trace the sentence.

Dancing can be fun!

Cross-curricular—Science

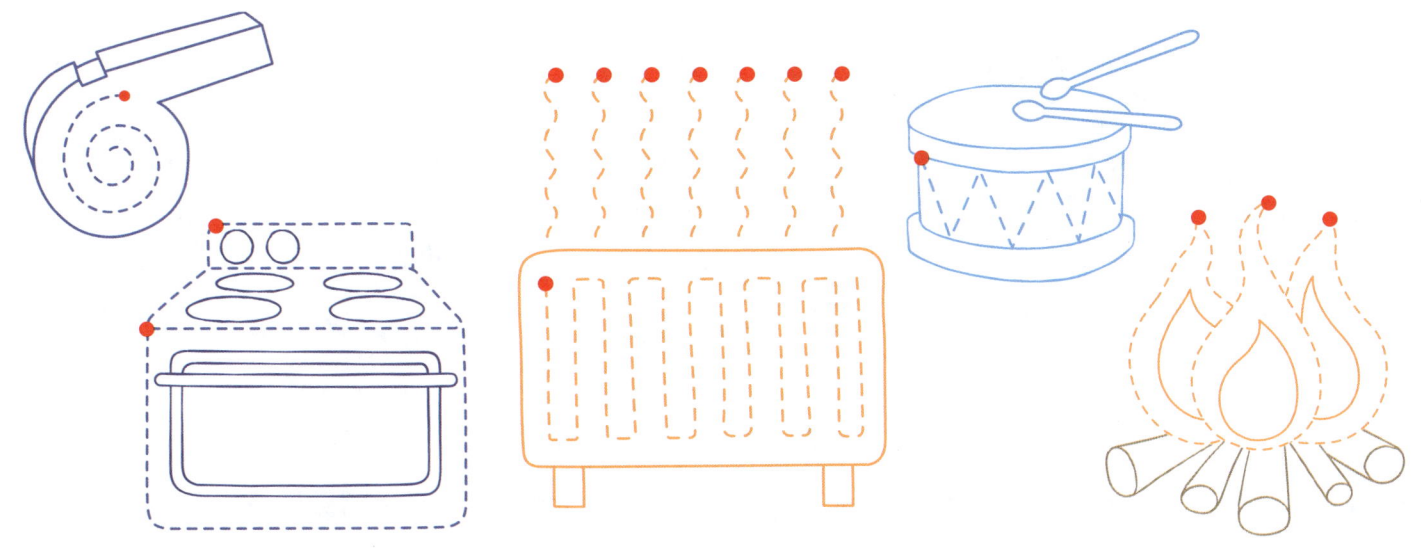

Trace, then sort the words into each column.

stove   recorder

drum   sun

guitar   campfire

heater   whistle

Objects That Make Heat	Objects That Make Sound

Cross-curricular—English

Trace, then copy the sentences with capital letters and full stops.

your mum is strong

their dad is playful

his cat is naughty.

her dog is friendly

my family is loving

Cross-curricular—History

Trace, then copy the sentences.

My grandparents played different

games when they were children.

They had different toys and

wore different clothes too!

They were young once.

Cross-curricular—Physical Education

Trace the sentences.

I can roll.

I can balance.

I can twist.

I can turn.

I can climb.

I can stretch.

I can change feet.

Trace, then copy the sentence.

I can move

on two hands

and two feet.

Draw one other way to move.

Trace, then copy the sentences.

My park has lots of trees

and soft grass.

It has swings and things

to climb.

It is a good place to play.

Read, trace and copy the poem.

Laura Lizard likes to play

In the sun on a hot day.

Laura is a happy girl.

She likes to sing and twirl.

I like Laura! Don't you?

Cross-curricular—English

Read and trace the words.

man
had
bat
red
mop
ten
hit
not
pin
bug
day
lip

Trace and complete the rhyming words.

___an
___ad
___at
___ed
___op
___en
___it
___ot
___in
___ug
___ay
___ip

Did you have any problems joining the letters? Yes No

Cross-curricular—Mathematics

Copy the number story.

Tom had three cars.

Bill had four cars.

How many cars altogether?

Trace the answer.

nine   seven   six

Trace the number story.

Jill had a bear, a book and a flower. How many things?

Trace the answer.

three   two   four